THE GOLDEN DAYS OF RADIO ONE

THE GOLDEN DAYS OF RADIO ONE

Hotshots, Big Shots and Potshots

David Hamilton

ASHWATER
PRESS

Also by David Hamilton
A FULHAMISH TALE

© **Copyright David Hamilton 2017**

First published in 2017

The right of David Hamilton to be identified as the author of this work has been asserted by him in accordance with the Copyright, Designs and Patent Act 1988.

Designed and published for David Hamilton by
Ashwater Press
68 Tranmere Road, Whitton, Twickenham, Middlesex, TW2 7JB

www.ashwaterpress.co.uk

Printed by The Dorset Press, Dorchester, England

ISBN 978-0-9927119-8-6

Contents

WONDERFUL RADIO ONE

DAVID HAMILTON began his broadcasting career on Forces Radio in Germany in 1959 where he presented one of the first programmes to feature rock 'n' roll. After five years broadcasting for BBC radio, he hosted two shows on the final day of the BBC Light Programme – Housewives Choice and Music Through Midnight. His first show for Radio One was Family Choice on 20 November 1967. He was given his own daily show in June 1973. Two years later the show was simultaneously broadcast on Radio Two, giving it the biggest listening audience of the day. At the end of 1977 the David Hamilton Show moved to Radio Two where it stayed until late 1986 when David quit after a disagreement over the station's music policy. David then moved to commercial radio where he worked for the next 30 years.

To date he has clocked up over 12,000 radio shows and by 2017 was hosting daily shows for The Wireless as well as regular broadcasts on his local station, BBC Sussex and BBC Surrey. His programme, The Million Sellers, has been broadcast on many stations in the UK and abroad.

In 2016 he embarked on a 50-theatre tour – David Hamilton's Rock 'n' Roll Back The Years – still running in 2017.

www.rocknrollbacktheyears.co.uk
www.davidhamilton.eu
www.facebook.com/groups/diddydavidhamilton

Big thanks to Ken Coton for his infinite patience and customary Ashwater thoroughness.

www.ashwaterpress.co.uk

Chapter 1

INTRO

What's the collective noun for a bunch of dj's? Could it be 'a gabble'? In the 50 years since Radio One launched on 30th September 1967 a lot of 'gabblers' have come and gone. But there was one group who enjoyed the station's golden years, the ones who were there in the early days when Radio One was Britain's only pop music station.

Back then there were no BBC local stations, no commercial stations, just Radio Luxembourg in the evenings with its dodgy signal. And pop music then appealed to all members of the family, from grandparents to grandchildren, the same families who sat round the television together on Thursday nights to speculate about what would be number 1 that week on Top Of The Pops hosted, naturally, by the Radio One dj's.

With absolutely no competition apart from the middle-of-the-road Radio Two, Radio One could be heard in virtually every home and every car in Britain. There were only three television channels and when they closed down, usually around midnight, millions turned over to the radio.

With no breakfast television, the radio breakfast show was the one all the dj's coveted. The BBC's method of audience research at the time was primitive, consisting mainly of ladies who approached people in the street (usually in London) to ask them what they had listened to the day before, but it's likely that peak time audiences could have been sixteen or seventeen million, figures that can only be dreamt of today with over

600 registered radio stations in the UK. For six years between 1967 and 1973 the BBC with its Radios One, Two, Three and Four had a monopoly of listening.

By 1973 Radio One was facing a problem. Commercial radio had been given the green light and the first stations, LBC (talk) and Capital (music), were due to open, both in London. For the first time BBC radio was losing its monopoly. Nobody knew how good the new stations would be. Unlike the BBC, they would be run by businessmen and would have to make money or they would go out of business.

In June 1973, four months ahead of the launch of the commercial boys, Radio One announced a new schedule and signed up a group of the biggest names on two-year contracts to stop them defecting. (Until then one year was the longest contract anyone had.) Whoever the commercial stations came up with – and soon they would mushroom around the country until there was one in every town and city – the Beeb would have the glamour boys, the ones you would read about in the newspapers and magazines and see on television, many who'd built their followings on the pirate ships in the Sixties. They were proven crowd pullers. When Tesco launched a new supermarket, the opening ceremony was performed either by a star of Coronation Street or a Radio One dj and huge crowds would turn up. They were recognisable faces, often appearing on panels of television shows like Blankety Blank, Punchlines and Celebrity Squares. Stories about them cropped up regularly in the tabloids. Some became better known than the stars whose records they played.

So a batch of household names was there to stop those enormous audiences dwindling away. No one knew then that the fight would get nasty and dirty. But for sure the battle was on, and Radio One would field its First Eleven.

Chapter 2

ROCK 'N' ROLL IS HERE TO STAY

When Bill Haley And His Comets played Rock Around The Clock in the film The Blackboard Jungle, teenagers jived in the aisles and some even ripped up the cinema seats. Rock 'n' Roll is here to stay, sang Danny And The Juniors, and it was – the music for the first generation growing up after World War II. Until then we'd had our parents' music – songs like How Much Is That Doggie In The Window? and Feet Up, Pat Him On The Po Po, and crooners like Bing Crosby and Peggy Lee. Rock 'n' Roll had energy, it had zest, it made you want to get up and dance. Apart from Haley, the man with the kiss curl on his forehead, the main exponents were Little Richard, the bible punching Richard Penniman, who gave us Good Golly Miss Molly, Tutti Frutti and Long Tall Sally; Jerry Lee Lewis, the man nicknamed 'The Killer' whose party piece was to play the piano while he was standing on it and treated us to such classics as Great Balls Of Fire and Whole Lotta Shakin' Goin' On; Chuck Berry and Elvis Presley.

Chuck Berry's songs were loved and recorded by the Beatles and the Stones. Rock 'n' Roll Music was one of his hits, and his name was synonymous with the genre. He was such a clever writer that he sold the same song twice to the record buying public with different lyrics and different titles. School Day was number 24 in the UK charts in 1957 and No Particular Place To Go number 3 in 1964. When he died, aged 90, in March 2017, all the rock stars cited him as their inspiration and an old John Lennon quote was recalled, 'If you tried to give rock 'n' roll another name, you might call it Chuck Berry.'

As to the man they called The King, Elvis Presley, listen to his early tracks now and, despite the primitive recording techniques of the day, the extraordinary quality of his voice shines through. To put his popularity in perspective, he sold over a billion records.

At last the generation we now call the post war baby boomers had its own music. The trouble was the BBC ignored it. The few record shows they had were presented by former band leaders like Jack Payne and Jack Jackson. They had been together in the BBC Dance Orchestra in 1931 and were steeped in big band music. In fairness to Jackson, with his Record Roundup which he started in 1948 and later recorded at his home in Tenerife, he pioneered a new style of presentation, punctuating records with clips from comedy classics, something that would inspire future broadcasters like Kenny Everett and Adrian Juste. Who could forget his opening chant "Ooh, it's Sunday!…"

The big show of the week on the BBC Light Programme was Two Way Family Favourites, a request show for forces serving abroad. Some weeks it branched out to outposts like Aden and Cyprus and occasionally even to Australia and New Zealand, but mainly it was a link up between the BBC studios in London and the studio of the British Forces Network in Cologne. It was said to be the only radio show with its own smell. When you heard the opening theme, With A Song In My Heart played by Andre Kostelanetz, at Sunday lunchtime you could smell the roast beef and Yorkshire pudding that was cooking in millions of households around the country. At its peak it was the programme on which the presenters, Cliff Mitchelmore and Jean Metcalfe, met and married – a true radio romance. Jean was in London, Cliff in Cologne and to think his chat up line was, "What's the weather like today, Jean?" Looking back, there was something very comfortable and comforting about it, but it didn't do the trick for us teenagers who would have to sit through three records we didn't like very much to hear one that was remotely 'pop'. And Cliff Richard singing Move It would be the nearest we'd get to rock 'n' roll.

And so we turned in the evenings to Radio Luxembourg, a commercial station based in the Grand Duchy of Luxembourg with a signal bounced across the sea and aimed at an audience in the UK on 208 metres on the medium wave. Coming from so far away the signal wasn't great. It was better after dark but, especially on summer evenings, we'd sit close to the radio, constantly twiddling the knob as the signal came and went. Luxembourg brought us the Ovaltineys and Horace Bachelor, the man who would predict football results with his Infra Draw Method based in Keynsham, 'spelt K-E-Y-N-S-H-A-M', Bristol. But most of all it brought us rock 'n' roll. And it brought a new job description into the English language – 'disc-jockey'.

Imported, like rock 'n' roll, from the USA, the term was first coined in 1935 by American radio commentator Walter Winchell when referring to a colleague who would 'jockey', i.e. operate the machinery that played the disc. The first time I heard it used was on Radio Luxembourg in the mid-Fifties where the resident disc-jockeys were Peter Madren and Pete Murray. Madren had a nice voice and an easy style but Murray was undoubtedly the star turn. He was witty in a cheekie chappie kind of way – a sort of Max Miller of music radio. As an actor, he introduced a series of voices to his shows. One character who appeared was 'Mabel' who didn't say much.

Her main contribution was to let out a little cry when Pete uttered one of his double entendres. He'd play a record called Sea Cruise by Frankie Ford and follow it with the expression 'up periscopes' at which Mabel's high pitched voice would go "Oooooh…" as though she'd been goosed, or it would be Brenda Lee and Here Comes That Feeling and "Oooooh", off she'd go again. As a dedicated listener, it didn't take me long to realise that Pete was the voice of Mabel.

Like most teenagers of my era, obsessed with the new found novelty of sex, Pete's earthy jokes were just the kind of humour I wanted to hear and I felt really grown up knowing what he was on about. There was also something rather naughty about listening to Radio Luxembourg. As with the pirate stations in years to come, there was the feeling that because it came from somewhere else, not the UK, you shouldn't really be listening to it.

But what did our heroes look like and did the faces match the voices? One way to find out was through FAB 208, the magazine named after the Luxembourg wavelength. There in one edition was Pete Murray looking handsome and tall in the saddle, horse riding in the Grand Duchy. What a glamorous job he had, thought this impressed teenager – horse riding and answering his fan mail by day and playing records at night. By the late Fifties Pete had married a Luxembourg girl and returned to the UK where in 1957 he became the host of the first ever pop show on television. This was 6.5 Special which went out on BBC TV at, not surprisingly, five past six on Saturday nights to the strains of its theme tune recorded by Don Lang and his Frantic Five – "Over the points, over the points…" – and gave a break to many of the pop stars of the day. Pete opened the show with the words "It's time to jive on the old 6.5." Sounds corny now, but it was hip at the time.

Josephine Douglas co-hosted it along with Pete with frequent appearances from the boxer, Freddie Mills. Jack Good, the original producer, saw it to be purely a pop show, knowing that was what young people wanted, but the BBC insisted it should be partly a magazine programme. Good left for ITV where his programmes like Wham! and Oh Boy – strictly music shows – became ratings smashes. 6.5 Special finally hit the buffers at the end of 1958.

Despite its long run, only one edition of the show remains in circulation, according to Kaleidoscope, the television archivists. Pete, now in his nineties and still a class act on the golf course, says the one remaining show isn't a good example of the series – "Too much worthiness" – despite a lively interview between him and the zany Spike Milligan. Pete went on to host Thank Your Lucky Stars for ITV, until an Equity strike put paid to his appearances, and in 1964 he became one of the team of original hosts of the legendary music show, Top Of The Pops, along with Jimmy Savile, David Jacobs and Alan Freeman. Jacobs also introduced the long-running BBC series, Juke Box Jury, on which Murray was a regular panellist. It says a lot for the tolerance and lack of expectation from young people of the time that millions of us would sit watching a show that amounted to nothing more than shots of panellists and members of the studio audience listening to new records and the panel then deciding whether they would be a 'hit' or a 'miss'.

As with many after him, Pete Murray found that Radio Luxembourg provided a good springboard to working for the BBC. Although the BBC hated Radio Luxembourg and what it stood for, the Beeb had no qualms about hiring broadcasters who'd learned their craft in the Grand Duchy, while never actually finding and blooding any new talent themselves.

When dj's made the switch, either because they'd had enough of living in the sleepy atmosphere of Luxembourg or because they thought there were more opportunities back in the UK, they soon found the BBC Light Programme lacked the informality of the Luxy shows. Presenters were still expected to write scripts that had to be approved by the producer.

The other problem was 'needle time'. The Musicians Union had a very strong lobby to 'Keep Music Live'. This meant that, unlike Radio Luxembourg, the BBC could only play a limited number of records a day. In the Fifties, Light Programme listeners had been entertained by the 'Slow, slow, quick, quick, slow' ballroom sounds of Victor Silvester and the Latin rhythms of Edmundo Ros (a man who lived to 100 having spent much of his life broadcasting on the BBC, so obviously it did him no harm...). On Sundays after Family Favourites we had the Billy Cotton Band Show with Billy's familiar welcome, "Wakey, wakey!" All this was fine until rock 'n' roll came along and the public had acquired an insatiable appetite for records. By the Sixties the BBC was the biggest employer of musicians in the country with eleven house orchestras. Because of a long running agreement with the Musicians Union, the musicians were employed as members of BBC staff. In 1980 when the BBC, citing the need for economy cuts, attempted to axe five of its house orchestras – the Scottish Symphony Orchestra, Northern Ireland Orchestra, Midland Radio Orchestra, Northern Radio Orchestra and the London Studio Players – the Musicians Union called a strike. One could understand that over a hundred musicians would not want to relinquish what was rare in their industry – regular employment – but the fact was that public taste had moved on.

Early in the 1960s the Light Programme produced a series of hybrid programmes that offered listeners a mixture of current songs played by an orchestra like that of Joe Loss and sung by his resident singers, Rose Brennan and Ross McManus (father of Elvis Costello) with appearances by some of the pop acts of the day. My first radio broadcast in the UK in 1962 was as the host of The Beat Show featuring the BBC Northern Dance Orchestra. Recorded at the BBC's Playhouse Theatre in Hulme, Manchester, on a Monday night, it was broadcast at lunchtime the following Thursday on the Light Programme. I opened it with the words, "It's The Beat Show with Bernard Herrmann and the NDO, the band with the beat that's reet." Sadly, it wasn't that reet for an audience of teenagers who came along to scream at their pop idols like The Searchers and Wayne Fontana and the Mindbenders while tolerating with a bored air the efforts of the orchestra who were probably at their best when covering the recordings of Herb Alpert and the Tijuana Brass. I am grateful that The Beat Show gave me my first break in radio, but looking back I realise it was a compromise that finished up pleasing no one in particular except the most tolerant. But if you wanted to hear music there was nothing else to listen to.

By the mid-Sixties the Light Programme started to feature more music shows. Swingalong and Swing Into Summer were weekday shows hosted by a repertory of presenters who would each do a week at a time. The music played was a mixture of records plus recordings made at the BBC studios in Maida Vale. The number of staff involved was enormous. Apart from the producer and recording engineer in Maida Vale, there was the gang in the basement studio at Broadcasting House: the producer, the producer's secretary (complete with stopwatch to time everything), a 'grams' operator who would play the records, another engineer to play tapes and a studio manager who would open and close the faders that controlled the records, tapes and the presenter's microphone. The presenter who sat on the other side of the glass would have been sent a running order a week before so that he could write a script for the broadcast. If the show went out at 2pm, he'd be required to arrive at Broadcasting House at 11 in the morning to do a 'tops and tails' rehearsal. This would involve hearing the end of records, reading the script and then doing a 'voice-over' on top of the instrumental introduction of the next record and talking up to the vocal. After rehearsal there would be a break for lunch in the BBC Club. Since the presenter was freelance and keen to ingratiate himself with the producer it was sort of expected that he would buy lunch.

The first producer I worked with was Doreen Davies, a middle-aged lady whose husband, Derek Mills, was another producer. She was very encouraging to new talent and sat in the control room with a big smile on her face. When a voice-over went particularly well, she'd give me a big thumbs-up. If I crashed the vocal, she'd look tactfully at the floor. Crashing the vocal – talking over the singer – was the arch sin and led to a loss of confidence by the presenter who, employed once every few weeks, would fear he'd never be invited back – and there was nowhere else to go. Not all the producers were as understanding as Doreen. One man asked me over lunch if he could look at my script. "I notice you use the expression 'right now' a lot," he said. (It was an expression most presenters used.) "Is there another way you can say this? What about 'just now'? Or even 'now'. That's a good word, isn't it?"

"You don't like 'right now'?" I said.

"No."

That afternoon in the studio I suddenly heard myself say "right now". It was one I'd forgotten to cut out of my script. From the expression on his face I knew I'd committed the ultimate sin, worse even than crashing the vocal. Right now, I thought, I don't think I'll get invited back.

Fortunately I did, and finally came the chance to present what was a 100% record show, Midday Spin. My fee was 25 guineas – £26 + 5 shillings (£26.25) – and my contract read "To present at the microphone a selection of gramophone recordings to be chosen by the producer and broadcast on the BBC Light Programme." Though it was a record show, the production team on the other side of the glass remained the same with the exception of the tapes operator who wasn't needed this time. Overstaffing was rife and sometimes producers would say to me, "I won't be here next time. I'm off on a sabbatical." I'd never heard the expression before but I discovered that when staff had been working for the BBC for a certain number of years they were sent off on a six-month paid holiday.

Being on the staff at the BBC was a very cushy number in the Sixties. It was almost impossible to get the sack. Only bankruptcy or being caught with their trousers down in Hyde Park could lose staffers their jobs. That or taking a bribe for playing a record. That in itself was a grey area. The BBC bosses were well aware of the Payola scandal in America where dj's and producers were found to have taken backhanders for promoting certain artists. In a blaze of publicity dj Alan Freed (the man believed by many to have coined the term rock 'n' roll) and TV host Dick Clark were accused of taking inducements to play records on air. One dj from Chicago admitted taking 22,000 dollars to play a record. To ensure the same thing didn't happen here, it was decided at the BBC that the responsibility for choosing music should be kept in house and done by staff producers and not freelance broadcasters. The guidelines for producers here were: it was OK being taken out for lunch by a 'plugger' from a record company, being given records and tickets to a concert, receiving a bottle of booze at Christmas; not OK: getting free holidays, major presents (like cars), drugs or cash.

One senior producer was suspended when it was discovered that a record company gave him a free holiday in Malta in return for playing a Dorothy Squires record on Family Favourites. He was put on 'gardening leave' where he remained for years. His garden must have been the envy of his neighbours. Sadly, his life wasn't a bed of roses, because he never returned to work.

Safe though staff jobs may have been, they weren't that well paid. As music radio got bigger, producers were rubbing shoulders with dj's who were starting to make big money from TV appearances and gigs as well as with the stars whose records they were playing who were earning even more. To keep up with this lifestyle, some were living beyond their means. One producer caught me on the hop when he asked me to lend him the equivalent of what today would be £5,000. I couldn't say I didn't have it because he knew I was out doing gigs three nights a week. I suppose, too, that I wanted to curry favour with him because it was always a good thing to get along with producers you worked with. I lent him the money, which he promised to pay back within six months. A year went by, and still no money. When I bumped into him, I felt embarrassed (God knows why) and he didn't bat an eyelid. Eventually, I had to write to him and tell him the next letter would come from my solicitor. He paid the money back. Sometime afterwards I was at a dinner party where another guest was the owner of a big record company. We got talking about the BBC and how poorly the producers were paid. I told the story of the loan but declined to name the producer.

"I'll tell you who it was," said the record company man, and promptly came up with the correct name.

"How did you know?" I asked.

"Because he asked me for money and I gave him £10,000."

"Gave it to him? Why?"

"Because when I wanted records played I knew he'd put them in his shows."

I harked back to the programmes I'd presented with this particular producer and remembered thinking at the time, some of these records are really dodgy and why are we playing them?

Sometime after our conversation the producer was put in charge of the one and only radio programme that gave away money. It turned out to be a lethal combination. Many months down the line it was discovered that every week he invented a bogus contestant and pocketed the money himself. No gardening leave this time. The BBC bosses reported him to the police and he went to prison. I never discovered what it was that caused his money problems but clearly keeping up with the showbiz lifestyle didn't help.

By the early Sixties the BBC was still enjoying a monopoly in radio listening. Although commercial television (ITV) had launched in 1955 and was described by Lord Thomson of Fleet, the newspaper magnate, as 'a permit to print money', there was still no legalised commercial radio in Britain and the BBC had no rival to keep it on its toes. Successive governments had thwarted any attempts to give commercial radio the go-ahead but a group of businessmen came up with the idea of broadcasting from international waters off the coast of Britain. Three miles away from the British coast and they were beyond the jurisdiction of the government. First off the mark was Ronan O'Rahilly, an Irish businessman with music business connections. One of the people he'd recorded on his independent record label was Georgie Fame. Trying to get his record played proved difficult. When approaching the BBC he discovered the record industry was dominated by EMI and Decca. Similarly, he found that most Radio Luxembourg shows were sponsored by EMI, Decca, Pye and Phillips. The only way to get his record played, he reasoned, was to start his own radio station.

In February 1964 he acquired a former Danish passenger ferry, Fredericia, and converted it into a radio ship in the Irish port of Greenore. He re-named her Caroline after Caroline Kennedy, daughter of US President John F. Kennedy (Neil Diamond recorded Sweet Caroline in her honour), and moored her off the coast of Felixstowe in Suffolk. Radio Caroline began broadcasting on 28 March 1964, opened by Simon Dee.

Within months there were two Radio Carolines. The original ship sailed away and anchored off the coast of the Isle Of Man, becoming Radio Caroline North, while a new ship – the MV Amigo – became Radio Caroline South and broadcast from off the coast of Frinton-on-Sea in Essex. Between them they covered most of the country, and in their wake came a series of pirate stations, some broadcasting from ships and others from disused forts. By 1967 there were ten such pirate stations. Radio London, one of the most successful, hit the airwaves at Christmas 1964 and included in its team a zany nineteen-year-old called Kenny Everett. His show with Dave Cash – Kenny and Cash – achieved cult status. A major coup was when Tony Blackburn defected from Radio Caroline.

Unaffected by the 'needle time' restrictions that hampered the BBC, the pirate stations were able to give young people what they wanted – the latest records that they were buying in the shops played by unscripted, ad-lib personality dj's. There was the added cachet that in listening to them you were doing something rather naughty, not to say illegal. They reflected the mood of the Swinging Sixties.

The government of the day broke a million hearts when they brought in the Marine Broadcasting Offences Act in August 1967, making it illegal for offshore pirate radio stations to broadcast if they were operated or assisted by people subject to UK laws, and also to carry water or goods to the ships. One by one the stations closed down. Still reluctant to introduce land based commercial radio stations in the UK, the government decided that instead it would ask the BBC to re-structure its networks – then comprising The Light Programme, Home Service and Third Programme – and replace them with three new services, one of which would play pop music – yes, even rock 'n' roll.

Chapter 3

THE PIRATE WHO RAN AGROUND

The pirate who made the biggest impact was Simon Dee. Carl Henty-Dodd, to give him his real name, was the first voice to be heard on Radio Caroline when it launched in 1964. With the writing on the wall for the pirates, he joined the BBC and presented Midday Spin, the show that, as it turned out, was used to showcase the talents of what would be the new breed of dj's on Radio One. The reason he wasn't in that original line-up photographed on the steps of All Souls Church was that he had a more important assignment. Bill Cotton, head of Light Entertainment at BBC TV, had signed him up to spearhead his peak time chat show. Saturday nights kicked-off with Dee Time complete with an opening film montage of Simon arriving in his E-type Jaguar accompanied by a glamorous blonde. Sadly, that was probably the best part of the programme.

Simon was completely untrained in television technique and appeared not to be the sort of person who would take kindly to advice. He seemed not even to grasp the basic principle that the camera with the red light on it was the one he should be addressing. Consequently he was often wrong camera'ed and, even when that would have been apparent to most people, he continued playing to the wrong camera, as though the director should be following him and not the other way round. Sometimes he would click his fingers and say, "Give me a camera." He was literally calling all the shots.

Such was his confidence and panache that he made Jonathan Ross, who followed in his wake years later, seem like a shy, retiring wallflower.

Two years later when he left the BBC for a hefty price rise and a two-year contract at ITV, few at the BBC missed him. It wasn't long before everything went wrong at the commercial station as well. Towards the end of his unhappy run he went through four producers in four weeks, each of them refusing to work with him again.

The last of the four was one of the station's senior producers, Bryan Izzard. Matters came to a head when Dee was interviewing the English actress, Jean Simmons. Izzard had noticed that Simmons was swinging her leg and kicking the desk, making the microphone reverberate. He buzzed through to the telephone on the desk to ask Dee to tell her to stop. Viewers saw Dee pick up the telephone and say, "Yeh, yeh. How very boring." He replaced the receiver, said nothing to the actress and the reverberating continued through the interview. At the end of the show as the audience was filing out, Izzard strode into the studio, picked up Dee by the lapels of his jacket and said, "Next time I tell you to do something, bloody well do it."

A meeting was arranged between the two men the following week in an attempt to restore some harmony. Unfortunately, it had the opposite effect. After a few minutes, Izzard said, "I've tried hard to get on with you, Simon, but you are without doubt a jumped-up, horrible little twit." To which Dee replied, "And Bryan, you are a fat old queen." Straight out of How To Win Friends And Influence People. So that was the end of Simon Dee at ITV. He blamed everything on David Frost, saying Frost had booked all the biggest stars for his show, leaving him with the also-rans. With BBC and ITV the only television networks of the day, Simon Dee had run out of stations to work for.

He was still a big name and there remained the lucrative market of personal appearances which he could have plundered for some time to come, but he even managed to blow that. Carl Gresham was a leading agent at the time, who specialised in booking artistes for personal appearances. A former extra in Coronation Street, he had formed friendships with stars like Bill Roache and Pat Phoenix. He found that, like many other actors from the Street, they were more than keen to supplement the wages they earned from Granada by pressing the flesh and signing autographs at the opening of bingo halls, supermarkets, fetes and carnivals. 'The Gresh', as he called himself, enjoyed rubbing shoulders with the stars and often accompanied them on their gigs. A girlfriend of mine nicknamed him 'Mr Cash Register Eyes' and noticed that at the mention of money he would rub his hands in glee, his eyes would bulge and he'd go red in the face.

In 1972 Woolworth had refurbished many of their stores and had asked Gresham to book stars to appear at the re-openings around the UK. Let The Gresh tell the story…

"I booked 39 stars to appear at various Woolies stores on the same day. Some appeared at more than one store. There was Bob Monkhouse, Hughie Green from Opportunity Knocks, Frazer Hines from Emmerdale, Tony Blackburn and David Hamilton and many more. Bar one, every celebrity turned up on time.

"The only one who didn't show up was Simon Dee. There was a huge crowd waiting outside the store he was due to open in Belfast. Fifteen, thirty minutes went by after the opening time and the crowd was getting restless. Half an hour later the manager was handed a telegram. With trembling hand he opened it and then said to the crowd, "Ladies and gentlemen, we don't have Simon Dee, but we do have a telegram from him." With that, he read out the telegram which said, "The day you people learn to live in peace together will be the day that I, Simon Dee, will come to Northern Ireland." The manager had a near riot on his hands.

"Simon might have lost his television shows but he could have made a lot of money from personal appearances for a long time to come. Instead of earning a good fee and fulfilling an obligation, he wanted to teach the people of Northern Ireland a lesson. After that I never used him again."

For Simon it was the start of the slippery slope. There were various attempts at a comeback. Radio 210, based in Reading, offered him a daily radio show and there was much publicity when Simon accepted. On the eve of the first show, the producer rang him and said, "Simon, we're looking forward to seeing you tomorrow and we've got Alvin Stardust as your first guest."

"You must understand," said Dee, "I always choose my own guests."

"That's fine," said the producer. "After the show we can sit down and draw up a list of people you'd like but for tomorrow we've got Alvin Stardust."

"You can have your Mr Starbright," said Dee, "but you won't be having me."

Everything Simon did continued to make newspaper headlines for many years, but little of it earned him any money apart from what he got from signing on at Fulham Labour Exchange. Radio Two did offer him a comeback on Sounds of the Seventies but he fell out with them because he refused to do the shows from Bristol. He went to prison for vandalising a lavatory seat with Petula Clark's face on it.

Ironically, the magistrate who sentenced him was his old BBC boss, Bill Cotton.

The last time I saw him was in a restaurant in Sheen. He was at an adjoining table and I overheard him boasting to his dining companions that he was doing a new series for TVS, the ITV station based in Southampton. I was working for TVS at the time and mentioned the conversation to the gang there a few days later. They assured me there were no plans to use Simon Dee.

The Simon Dee story was a lesson to us all. The lesson was that no matter how big a star is, if they're difficult to work with they can be gone overnight. In Simon's case, maybe it wasn't entirely his fault. Perhaps he was given too much too soon, before he was ready to handle it. After just a few heady years, the biggest of the pirates sank without trace.

Chapter 4

WONDERFUL RADIO ONE

The arrival of the pirates at Broadcasting House caused quite a shock. Those who joined en masse at the station's launch in September 1967 were looked on with disdain by the pin-striped brigade in the BBC Club. Many of them had long hair and wore beads. One was known as 'The Marshal' and wore a stetson and cowboy boots. No one like them had been seen before in the BBC Club.

There were some leftovers from the old Light Programme. Pete Murray, a youthful looking 44, would soon move to Radio Two, his natural home where he could play more of the music he liked. Jimmy Young, two years older than Pete, was the surprise choice for the morning slot, the one the 'housewives' listened to. As well as his cookery tips – "What's the recipe today, Jim?" – he also sang songs he recorded in the BBC studios, an unusual ingredient since his highly successful singing career (number 1 in the charts with Unchained Melody and The Man From Laramie) was ended by the advent of rock 'n' roll.

Although the old staffers viewed them with great suspicion, some of the ex-pirates would forge a long-running career at Radio One. Others defected to commercial radio some years later, finding it a home more akin to the pirates. One lasted just one show before the bosses decided they didn't like what he did. Though everybody tried to make the best of it, the union between the BBC and music radio was not an easy one and still the 'needle time' problem remained. The 'Keep Music Live' lobby was going strong and, although the BBC was constantly negotiating to play more records, the Musicians Union insisted that a large percentage of Radio One's output should consist of recordings made at the BBC, either by house orchestras or by groups and bands making cover versions of their records. Bearing in mind that many hours of painstaking work were done in cutting a disc, what was done in limited time in BBC studios could never compare with the original. Listeners with a good ear for music could easily tell the difference between the actual record and a poor copy. In the end, it was all about compromise. The perception of the majority of listeners at the start was that Radio One wasn't as good as the pirate stations, there was still resentment that they had been outlawed, but this is all there is, so let's make the best of it. The BBC hoped that having the ex-pirates on board would soften the blow and that their popularity would keep the listeners happy.

One good thing was that the scripted, formal type of broadcasting of the Light Programme had gone out of the window. Everything was now much more relaxed, and with dj's in a regular daily spot, instead of the 'repertory' system, they didn't have to worry so much about not being invited back. Crashing the vocal was no longer a heinous crime. One dj did it and said to the vocalist on the record, "Do you mind not singing while I'm trying to speak?" Gone, too, was the large team of production people on the other side of the glass. As in the style of the pirates, the dj was virtually a one man band, playing all the records, jingles and tapes himself with just a technical operator next door keeping an eye on volume levels.

There's no doubt that the period between the launch of Radio One and the opening of the first commercial stations almost exactly six years later in 1973 was the golden age of music radio, if not for the listeners then certainly for the dj's. Whereas today every town and city has the choice of several commercial stations as well as a local BBC one, then there was only Radio One. Its 247 metres medium wave signal boomed in loud and clear to almost every part of the UK It was the time of the transistor radio. People took their trannies to work, to the beach and into the park to listen to while they had their sandwiches at lunchtime. The agreement between Radio One and BBC TV was that only Radio One dj's would be used as hosts of Top Of The Pops, so they became recognisable faces as well. Wherever they went on personal appearances, they'd meet people who would talk to them about things they'd said that day. Radio audiences were enormous because there was no competition.

Fifteen million was a figure banded about, or sixteen million, or seventeen depending on which newspaper you read. Nobody really knew how many people were listening because the BBC system of research was fairly haphazard. It consisted of a group of ladies who would go out into the streets (probably mainly in London) and ask people which programmes they listened to and for how long. They also asked – and this was an important criterion for the BBC – how much they appreciated the programmes they were listening to. The programmes that usually got the highest appreciation index, though not necessarily the biggest audience, were the specialist programmes transmitted during the evening. Well, they would, wouldn't they? Someone listening to a country music show would obviously enjoy country music.

The method of audience research was thrown into serious doubt when Margaret Thatcher, the prime minister, was due to appear on the Jimmy Young Show. The questions asked were:

Did you find the interview with Margaret Thatcher (1) very interesting, (2) interesting, or (3) not interesting? Most people answered (1) very interesting, which was very interesting because on the day of the broadcast Margaret Thatcher didn't turn up. Research was then done into the researchers which showed that on the day in question it had been raining hard and it was probably easier for the ladies to decide among themselves that most people would find an interview with Margaret Thatcher 'very interesting'.

Radio One didn't have to worry too much about listening figures. With no one to sell advertising time to, they could jog along quite happily in the knowledge that they had a captive audience who had no other choice of listening. Wonderful Radio One, as the slick new jingles proclaimed it, ruled the airwaves. It was a very happy time for the disc-jockeys. With no ratings to worry about, it was probably the most secure time any presenters would ever enjoy in radio. Each one of them was a household name and much in demand for shop openings, beauty contests and carnivals. Some appeared in pantomime alongside established actors. Then there was the emerging new form of entertainment – the disco. Radio One dj's were a major attraction. Some developed a stage act, sometimes involving lights and go-go dancers. Even those that didn't have an act could earn good money. All was going swimmingly until in 1973 the go-ahead was given to legalised land based commercial radio. The senior service had finally caught up with television which had gone commercial 18 years earlier.

In June 1973 Radio One made wholesale changes to its line-up: Noel Edmonds on breakfast; Tony Blackburn with a three-hour show in the morning; Johnnie Walker at lunchtime; David Hamilton with a three-hour show in the afternoon. The team were charged with hanging on to Radio One's audience and not losing it to the new commercial stations. The first, Capital Radio (music) and LBC (talk), were due to open in London in October. Others would follow in towns and cities around the UK.

Initially, the BBC bosses were extremely complacent. Derek Chinnery, the head of Radio One, had worked his way up through the ranks, starting straight from school as a trainee at the age of sixteen. He went on to become an engineer and producer of shows featuring the likes of David Jacobs and Pete Murray, whose late night show Pete's Party was one of the most listened to shows on the Light Programme. Now he was in charge of a network playing the chart music of the day at a time when the public's musical taste was constantly changing. The Seventies brought along glam rock and later punk. "Radio One has the stars," he said, "the glamour boys who are on TV and are household names. The commercial people will never compete with us."

Soon after Capital Radio launched in October 1973, he and his colleagues got a shock. At a programme meeting someone noticed that Capital Radio stickers were appearing in cars all over London. Someone had heard that a squad of Capital Radio 'sticker spotters' were operating in the capital. If they spotted your sticker and read out your number plate on air, they would fill your car with petrol. It was irresistible and something the BBC couldn't do because they couldn't be seen to be spending licence payers' money. The next thing that became apparent was that Capital's motoring news was purely for London whereas Radio One, being a national station, had to cover traffic news for England, Scotland, Northern Ireland and Wales. Thus news of traffic hold-ups in Sauchiehall Street in Glasgow was of no interest to listeners in London, in the same way that news of delays in the Old Kent Road was of no interest to listeners in Glasgow. The other thing that swiftly became clear was that the commercial stations were run by businessmen who realised that the survival of their stations depended on them converting a large number of listeners, whereas the people working for the BBC had no experience of business at all.

One by one after London, every town and city would have its own commercial station and they started to mushroom all over the country. BRMB in Birmingham, Piccadilly Radio in Manchester, Radio City in Liverpool, Radio Tees in the North East, Radio Clyde in Glasgow, and so it went on. Each one would concentrate on its own patch with local sport, local news and local weather. Imagine the delight of listeners in Glasgow who would now hear Scottish voices pronouncing local place names correctly instead of dj's in London getting them all wrong and crowing about 'a lovely, sunny day' when in Scotland it was pouring with rain. What's more, the commercial boys didn't have the 'needle time' problems of Radio One and could play records for most of the day. And they played against the BBC's weaknesses. When Radio One had a six-minute segue recorded by Johnny Arthey, his orchestra and singers at 3 o'clock in the afternoon, Roger Scott opened his show on Capital Radio with Three O'Clock Thrill and went straight into three stonking great records.

Radio One's trump card was its star dj's and for the first time the corporation signed them up on two-year contracts – 'golden handcuffs' to stop them defecting to the commercial sector. Some like Dave Cash, David Symonds and Kenny Everett had already gone. Kenny was always a dangerous fit for the straight-laced BBC. They tore up his contract after he said on air, "When we were a kingdom, we were ruled by a king. When we were an empire, we were ruled by an emperor. Now we're a country, we're ruled by Margaret Thatcher." On Capital Radio he was much more at home introducing Dolly Parton's Biggest Hits. (Say it quickly...)

Radio One sent its jocks out on the road as often as possible. In the summer the Radio One Roadshow was enormously popular. On a good day it was commonplace to see 5,000 or more packed on a beach watching nothing more than a dj playing records and games like 'Bits and Pieces' and 'Guess the Mileage with Smiley Miley'. (Years later bands playing live were brought in to bolster the dwindling crowds.) Somewhat cynically, the bosses sent in a dj to do a roadshow in a town or city where a commercial station was about to launch, thereby upstaging it. Sometimes this backfired badly. The Ipswich Evening Post noted that a visit to the town just ahead of the opening of Radio Orwell was the first that Radio One had bothered to make for many years, and could that be purely coincidence? It did beg the question that Ipswich was one of those pockets where Radio One reception was very poor and the station could barely be heard. Needless to say, Radio Orwell was on a winner.

Things got quite hostile, too. In one Northern city I was asked by a commercial station rival, "What are you doing in our area?" I could have replied, "This is our area, too." In Bradford a BBC Outside Broadcast vehicle had its tyres let down. Suspicion fell on the local commercial station.

It didn't take the BBC too long to realise that local radio had a lot going for it and that the only way to take the commercial people on was to play them at their own game. A dozen new BBC local stations opened in the Seventies and amazingly we were often asked to mention and promote them at Radio One. It's hard to think of any other business that would invite its customers to go elsewhere. Even more amazingly, in 1974 Radio One allowed an internal enquiry to leak to the press. It included comments that many of its presenters were 'smug', 'patronising' and 'not popular with a large chunk of listeners'. Imagine Coca Cola or Mars allowing that to happen to their product. Talk about shooting yourself in the foot!

By the mid-Seventies most towns and cities in Britain had a commercial radio station and generally they were making money. Still, most presenters on them aspired to get to Radio One. That was the Premiership of radio where the dj's were national names and faces, often seen on television, who could earn big money from appearances in clubs and discos the length and breadth of Britain. Which brings us to our cover picture, as Radio One paraded its stars in its biggest line-up of all time in 1976.

Let's meet them and see how they have fared since those heady days...

Chapter 5

STEWPOT, THE KIDDIES' CHOICE

When Radio One launched in October 1967, there was one show no one wanted. While all the dj's wanted to be playing the sharpest, grooviest chart hits of the day, who would want to be introducing Nellie The Elephant and Sparky's Magic Train Set on the kids' programme, Junior Choice?

Before long someone offered to become the kiddies' favourite – Ed Stewart, a man clever enough to calculate that here was a market he could corner where nobody was likely to stab him in the back and invade his territory and on which he could go on and on for years doing nothing more taxing than reading out requests for children – as indeed he did. What's more it led to his own children's television series and to a long spell of hosting Crackerjack, the kids' TV show. Crackerjack. (Sorry, I just had to repeat that. Force of habit.) In fact, he did it for over twelve years until the controller of Radio One ousted Tony Blackburn from his daily show and gave him Ed's two weekend editions of Junior Choice, a move that made Tony about as happy as it made Ed.

Back in the early days of Radio One, Ed followed in the footsteps of Uncle Mac, the nickname of a BBC institution called Derek McCullough (a man later to be exposed by John Simpson as a paedophile who preyed on young boys who visited Broadcasting House). An avuncular figure indeed!

Ed himself acquired a nickname, Stewpot, and his party piece which he delivered at the drop of a hat involved opening his shirt and exposing his ample belly which he then rolled up and down like a roller coaster. (Yes, not a pretty sight.)

I got to know Ed well when we played together in a charity football team called The Top Ten XI. Ed was the goalkeeper but insisted on taking any penalties we were lucky to get. This involved him running the entire length of the field, while we stood around like lemons, and invariably crashing the ball against the bar which resulted in him scurrying back to his goal while we frantically ran around like blue-arsed flies trying to get into another goalscoring position.

Ed was also the captain of the team and always in the centre circle before kick-off to have his photo taken with a beauty queen for the local newspaper. His real name was Mainwaring (pronounced Mannering) so at last he achieved his ambition to become a Captain Mainwaring, though I have to say he was far from a 'stupid boy'. In fact he was quite shrewd and certainly canny with money.

There was a rumour that every pound he earned had been taken prisoner. His renowned tightness provided wonderful fodder for the other dj's to do 'meanie' jokes about him on air. Jokes like: "What's the difference between Ed Stewart and a coconut?" The answer: "You can get a drink out of a coconut." Or: "If Ed invites you to his home, not only do you take your own Scotch but your own rocks as well."

Stewpot didn't worry about this reputation. On the contrary, he seemed to revel in being the butt of his colleagues' humour.

When Ed was young and single he was quite a ladies' man and for some time dated the Hammer actress Ingrid Pitt and also New Seekers vocalist Eve Graham. In 1970 he and I were booked as mc's when speedway racing returned to Wembley Stadium. Bob Danvers Walker, for many years the voice of

Pathé News, had been hired as announcer. Bob still had that wonderful voice but he was getting on in years and found it difficult to keep up with the results and scores and didn't last long. But Ed and I enjoyed the rest of the season, and on the final day, after a match between Great Britain and the Rest of the World, we took part in a race with pop stars Leapy Lee, who'd just had a big hit with Little Arrows, and Troy Dante. I'd never ridden a motor bike before and for us to slide around the shale on high powered speedway machines with no brakes was an act of madness that could only be carried out by the young and foolish.

During that summer I had a girlfriend I was living with who thought Ed treated his girlfriend badly – in an off-hand way, with a sort of 'treat 'em mean and keep 'em keen' attitude – and I tended to agree with her, so one day I passed on my thoughts to Ed. "You do it your way," said Ed, "and I'll do it mine." A while later when my relationship was over and his was still going, I felt perhaps he had a point.

Having enjoyed the bachelor days, Ed married the daughter of the music publisher and sometime television show host, Jimmy Henney, and in doing so not only acquired a beautiful young wife but also a father-in-law who understood show business and how it worked and pointed Ed very much in the right direction. Henney had founded the first showbusiness football team, the Showbiz XI, and was also heavily into the golfing and charity scene. He showed Ed that the Vaudeville Golfing Society and the Water Rats were wonderful organisations for networking and that through them he could meet many influential figures in the business who could put work his way and also enjoy many free dinners, two advantages Ed found very appealing. It also tapped into Ed's sporty side. He was a good footballer, tennis and golf player and also cricketer.

In the radio studio Ed was an easy going character. He never let his work interfere with his love of sport and during his afternoon show at Radio Two he'd have the television on and would be watching the Test cricket or the tennis. We'd work in adjoining studios, and listening to his show while waiting to do mine I'd often hear a record come to an end and the needle start scratching on a groove in the middle. I'd press the talkback and say, "Ed, I think your record's ended." Through the glass between the studios I'd see him hurriedly put his headphones on and carry on as if nothing had happened. Because he didn't always listen to the records on his show he once played the non-broadcast version of the Beautiful South's Don't Marry Her which contained the lyrics, "Don't marry her, fuck me."

He also came badly unstuck when half reading an internal memo warning presenters not to do messages for some soldiers who had been killed in action in Northern Ireland. Not having digested the memo properly, he read out the names and then dedicated a record to them. There but for the grace of God could have gone many of us, but unfortunately it was Ed who made the gaff.

His long-running marriage came to an end when he discovered his wife was having an affair. There followed a bitter and costly divorce which cleaned him out.

But lucky Ed fell on his feet when he met an attractive Dutch widow called Elly. Elly took him under her wing and Ed had a smile on his face again. It goes to show that when you're at rock bottom, there's always hope...

Asked to make a speech at Ed's 70th birthday at a restaurant in Walton-on-Thames, I mentioned that in 50 years of knowing him – working at the same radio station, playing football, riding the speedway and partying together – I had never seen his wallet. With that he pulled it out. So, there was one after all! Yes, but it was on a chain hanging from his back pocket.

So we knew that Ed could take a joke. He was an affable character with an optimistic view on life. As he said, his glass was always half full – usually because someone else had filled it. Like the rest of us, he mellowed a lot. He was good company round a table at dinner or lunch. I saw a lot of him in recent years and spoke to him early in 2016 shortly after he'd done Junior Choice at Christmas for Radio Two. "I don't know if I'll be doing it this year," he said.

"Of course you will," I said. "You're an institution."

His words came back to haunt me. A few days later he died after a massive stroke at the age of 74. I miss him a lot.

A friend gave me an Ed Stewart wallet on a chain. Apparently, Radio Two with his blessing were giving them away as prizes. So Ed was in on the gag and played along with it; he wasn't really that tight after all. Although I did once see him swimming under a toll bridge.

Chapter 6

THE HAIRY CORNFLAKE

I have a confession to make. I gave Dave Lee Travis his nickname. We were doing a Radio One Club at the BBC's Paris Theatre in Lower Regent Street. Dave was on stage waiting to interview the Norwegian film actress, Julie Ege. I handed over to them and said, "Now – beauty and the beast. The beautiful Julie Ege and the Hairy Monster from 200 miles up the M1 motorway." Dave liked the moniker, and the 'Hairy Monster' he became, though some years later when he was given the breakfast show he, or someone in authority, changed it to the more cuddly 'Hairy Cornflake'.

I first met Dave when I was doing my first public appearances as a dj, playing records for the skaters on Monday nights at the Silver Blades ice rink in Manchester. He must still have been in his teens and had come along, I think, to see what the early disc-jockey sessions were like and how he might break into them.

His real name was David Griffin, though already he was calling himself Dave Lee Travis, which made him sound like a country singer. Though he was born in Buxton, he was based in Manchester and was hell bent on a career as a dj, inspired no doubt by the success of Jimmy Savile. My first impression of him was a man who oozed confidence with not a moment of self-doubt – perfect dj material! His big break came when he joined Radio Caroline and then producer John Wilcox brought him to the BBC as host of Pop North, one of the band shows recorded in Manchester where Dave delivered 'lunch with a punch'.

It wasn't too long before he was invited to London where Radio One worked him into their schedules. He appeared at almost every time of the day and every day of the week as the bosses shunted him around, finally landing the breakfast show in 1978. The breakfast show has always been regarded as the peak spot of the day. "Get lots of listeners early on and there's a knock-on effect for all the other presenters who come on later," is how one producer explained it to me. But it takes quite a toll on a presenter's life. Rising at 4 or 5am, depending on the starting time of the show, means either being in bed at 9 and turning down many social invitations or napping in the afternoon – depending on what works for each individual. Consequently, nobody hacks it for too long. Travis did it for three years before moving to afternoons.

Whatever time he broadcast he remained part of Radio One's schedule for 25 years, quite a feat in itself. He was a regular host of Top Of The Pops and even appeared as a performer on the show when his record Convoy GB hit number 4 in the charts. The record was a parody of CW McCall's Convoy, and was recorded with his pal Paul Burnett under the name Laurie Lingo and the Dipsticks. This really pissed off the commercial stations who had to play a record by two BBC dj's in their chart shows.

He also hosted for BBC TV The Golden Oldie Picture Show, introducing pop videos in a relaxed setting, smoking a pipe. One of his accolades was that he was voted Pipe Man of the Year. Another came along when he was the subject of This Is Your Life in 2000. For 20 years he presented A Jolly Good Show, one of the flagship programmes on the BBC World Service with its enormous worldwide audience.

DLT (or DOLT as Wogan once jokingly called him) was brilliant on the Radio One Roadshows and was one dj who came into his own at the disco gigs. With his extrovert personality he was well at home in front of audiences and put a lot into his shows, taking with him Froggy, his back-up dj, his personal assistant who was a former member of the pop group Pickettywitch, some dancers and a Darth Vader outfit which he wore on stage, cleverly changing the name to a dj term, Daft Fader. He liked his play on words, frequently referring to himself as a 'joss dickey'. His overheads were so big he can't have made much money from the shows but, fair play to him, his priority seemed to be more about everybody having a great time rather than him going home with bundles of cash in his pocket. He went down particularly well at Young Farmers gigs and in the North of England.

So what kind of bloke was he? Tactile, for sure. A hugger of women and men. Since he was such a great bear of a man, when he hugged you, you knew you'd been hugged. A practical joker with an enormous laugh. A man adored by his mother. His was the only dj's mother I remember coming along to our events. She was a mini version of Dave. (Without the beard, of course.)

But at times he displayed a particularly thin skin. He more than anyone hated the send-ups of Smashey and Nicey (Paul Whitehouse and Harry Enfield), though they were generally considered to be based on Tony Blackburn and Alan Freeman or perhaps an amalgam of Radio One dj's. Travis got quite shirty about them and failed to see the joke. He felt they demeaned us all. He was probably right and I'm sure he became angrier when they started pinching some of the work that might otherwise be done by Tony or Jimmy Savile or even him.

The term 'Smashey and Nicey' stayed around in radio circles for a long time and was used disparagingly against cheesy dj's which all of us had been at that time to a certain extent. It didn't help Dave's cause, and when Radio One's controller, Matthew Bannister, decided to have a massive clear-out of the old brigade – probably too severe a cull in retrospect – Dave's time was up. He made a dramatic announcement on air that displayed his bitterness about his leaving and how things were being run at the BBC: "I want to put the record straight at this point and I thought you ought to know – changes are being made here which go against my principles and I just cannot agree with them." As a fellow performer I could sympathise with him because the same thing has happened to me. But he missed the point that at a station like Radio One things would always be changing, and younger, though not necessarily better, people would always come along.

My feeling is that professionally Dave's world came to an end when he left Radio One. He'd been such a mainstay of the station for so long that he'd be forgiven for thinking he had a permanent pass into Broadcasting House. His great ambition in life was to be a Radio One dj, he'd achieved it and he didn't want to let it go. After he left he went to Classic Gold whose studios were in Dunstable, not far from his home, and discovered that working for commercial radio was a different ball game. He found himself at loggerheads with a head of music from New Zealand who almost certainly didn't know as much as Dave about pop music in Britain but insisted on calling all the shots. In time Dave left and started working for his local BBC station.

When I was doing the breakfast show for Saga Radio, based in Birmingham, Ron Coles, the MD, asked me what I thought about getting a name dj to stand in for me while I was on holiday. When I agreed, the first name he suggested was that of the man who inspired me to go into radio in the first place, Pete Murray. Pete came to the studio but said he couldn't work the mouse and the computer. I told him it was easier than driving a car and that, after half an hour in the studio with me, he'd have the hang of it. But Pete was adamant he couldn't do it. Ron's next choice was DLT. Dave came up to Birmingham for the press photo call with me but only agreed to do the show on certain conditions. I was staying in a hotel in Birmingham four nights a week to do the show, but Dave insisted he did it from his own studio at home. Whereas I was happy to use the station's playlist, Dave was adamant he wanted to choose the records. I couldn't believe it – he was the stand-in and demanding more than the regular man. He got his wishes but unfortunately the line from his studio dropped out one morning, the show went off the air and the station didn't use him again.

Travis was working for the Magic AM network in the north of England when a terrific career opportunity came his way. Burmese pro-democracy leader Aung San Suu Kyi had spent fifteen years under house arrest, literally a captive audience to Dave's Jolly Good Show on the BBC World Service. Now she was coming to England to meet the man who kept her company during her ordeal. It was a terrific photo opportunity for Dave and the pictures were splashed across the national newspapers in 2011, prompting a visit to Dave and his wife Marianne's home from the Sunday Times journalist, Camilla Long. It was a day when things went horrendously wrong. She began her article by saying, "I spent 90 minutes with the former Radio One dj DLT and I don't think there's a part of my body he didn't grope." The article seemed to act as a catalyst for a series of events that followed.

Liz Kershaw said she'd been groped while on air in a BBC studio by a dj but refused to name the person involved thus planting suspicion on anyone who had worked with her. Vivien Creegor, the Sky newsreader, also complained that she'd been groped while working at the BBC and named the man as DLT. After that other women came forward and in November 2012 he was arrested. While he was on bail for what seemed like an eternity, Magic AM took him off air. There followed two trials which cost an estimated million pounds of taxpayers money and cost Travis personally a huge amount in legal fees. He lost his house, his reputation and his work prospects, and at the end of it all he was given a three-month suspended sentence for touching one woman.

It was a tragic end to what for so long had been a brilliant career. A Dave Lee Travesty.

Chapter 7

THE EMPEROR WHO RULED THE AIRWAVES

"My, my, my. Have mercy. I'm gonna blow your mind, baby." And he did. When the Emperor Rosko hit the airwaves of Wonderful Radio One with his slick American tones in 1967, BBC listeners had never heard anything like it before – unless they'd caught him already on Radio Caroline. He was probably the first American dj the BBC had ever employed, and at a time when much radio presentation was stilted his 'jive talk' was something refreshingly different for British audiences. Such was the shock effect of one of his first broadcasts on Radio One that it was followed by the straight-laced voice of the newsreader saying, "And now, the news in English."

His real name was Michael Pasternak, son of the legendary film producer Joe Pasternak. Joe had great success with musicals like The Great Caruso starring Mario Lanza and operettas like The Merry Widow and The Student Prince. Later he produced Where The Boys Are starring Connie Francis who had a hit with the theme song and Girl Happy which starred Elvis Presley. Clearly young Michael grew up in a showbusiness environment rubbing shoulders with the stars in Los Angeles. But if he came to England to seek fame and fortune it would probably be because of the closeness of his style to the American dj Wolfman Jack and his opportunities would have been limited in the USA. Here he was something completely different.

For many years he hosted Rosko's Round Table where recording stars and dj's would listen to new recordings on Friday evenings and discuss their merits or otherwise. But he was much more than just a radio jock. He was one of the first dj's to hit the discotheque scene that appeared in the Sixties. While other dj's were unsure what to do in front of a live audience – even though they were paid bundles of money to do so – Rosko pioneered a whole new form of roadshows, combining a lighting and sound system with go-go dancers and his own zany personality. That, along with the ability to pick the kind of music that would fill dance floors, made him much in demand in dance halls and discos around the UK. He even had a rider in his contract that the management would provide a bottle of Bourbon in his dressing room. It is reputed that he polished it off before he went on stage – a rumour he has never denied.

Rosko had a big personality and was virtually unflappable – except on one occasion when interviewing members of the audience at the Radio One Club in London. Bored with asking questions, he said to one girl, "Would you like to ask me a question?" To which the girl replied, "Yes, is Dusty Springfield a lesbian?" For once in his life the Emperor was speechless.

After years of great success in the UK, he left in 1976 to be with his father, who was ill. Since then he has been back from time to time and is often heard in various countries on shows recorded at the studio in his home in A Thousand Oaks, California. Rosko's LA Connection goes out on fifteen small stations in the UK as well as Geneva and Holland. Coast To Coast Country features modern country music and also enjoys an international audience. Though he never broadcasts in

Britain he is certainly not forgotten and Richard Curtis based the character The Count on Rosko in his film The Boat That Rocked. When he's in London he often hosts dinners for his dj pals, including the author, at the home of his agent, Cherry. Such evenings are always full of fun and laughter.

In 2010 he was given a place in the Radio Hall of Fame, a well deserved tribute. Though he dabbled in television, Rosko was a true radio man. Back in the States he might have been just another American voice, but here he was totally different from anyone before or since.

Actually, Rosko has had three voices. The one we hear on radio is quite different from the one we heard in the Sixties and Seventies. I can't think of any dj whose voice has changed more. The third one is his natural speaking voice which sounds nothing like the other two. Despite all this, there has only ever been one Emperor Rosko – and there always will.

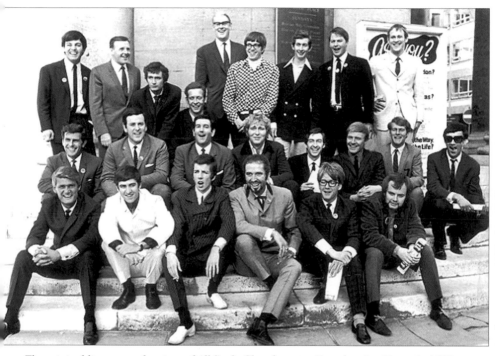

The original line-up on the steps of All Souls Church next to Broadcasting House in 1967.

Back row, left to right: Tony Blackburn, Jimmy Young, Kenny Everett, Duncan Johnson, Robin Scott, David Rider, Dave Cash, Pete Brady, David Symonds;

middle row: Bob Holness, Terry Wogan, Barry Alldis, Mike Lennox, Keith Skues, Chris Denning, Johnny Moran, Pete Myers;

front row: Pete Murray, Ed Stewart, Pete Drummond, Mike Raven, Mike Ahern, John Peel.

Where are they now? See the last page of the book.

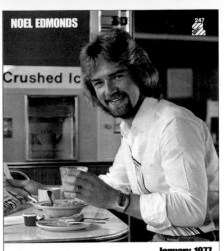

NOEL EDMONDS

January 1977

PAUL GAMBACCINI & KID JENSEN

February 1977

ALAN FREEMAN

March 1977

PAUL BURNETT

April 1977

SIMON BATES

May 1977

DAVID HAMILTON

June 1977

DAVE LEE TRAVIS

July 1977

ANNE NIGHTINGALE

LONDON   ALL OTHER PLACES

August 1977

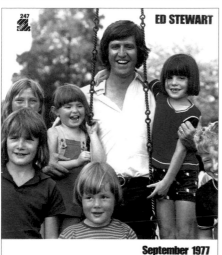

ED STEWART

September 1977

TONY BLACKBURN

October 1977

From the Radio One calendar for 1977. You may guess who was featured in November, which made it an easy decision for that page to be omitted here.

JOHN PEEL

December 1977

After a while manager Teddy Warrick (centre at back) strengthened the Radio One football team with some people who could actually play the game. Noel Edmonds, Paul Gambaccini, David Jensen, Paul Burnett and David Hamilton are joined by singers Junior Campbell and Miki Anthony, record pluggers Alan James and Dave Most and Radio One producer Jeff Griffin.

Johnnie Walker pops the question.

A 'gabble' of dj's on The One Show: Tony Blackburn, Trevor Nelson, David Hamilton, Mike Read and David 'Kid' Jensen.

Stuart Henry, as featured in Radio One's 1975 calendar.

The Philly fillies! The Three Degrees.

Pete Murray, an Arsenal supporter, has an away day by the Thames at Fulham Football Club.

Shades of Pete Murray in Luxembourg. Noel Edmonds, Tony Blackburn and David Hamilton horse riding in Hyde Park.

There won't ever be a radio station that has a line-up like Radio One did in 1976.

Standing, from left to right: Ed Stewart, Dave Lee Travis, Emperor Rosko, Alan Freeman, Anne Nightingale, John Peel, Johnnie Walker and Terry Wogan; front: David Hamilton, Noel Edmonds and Tony Blackburn.

Chapter 8

FLUFF FREEMAN

"Greetings, pop pickers," he began his programmes, and he closed them with, "All right, stay bright." In between there were plenty of 'not 'arfs'. A man of many catchphrases, Alan Freeman spoke in staccato tones and didn't say much on air but what he said was slick, punchy and sounded great, his voice deepened by the sixty cigarettes he smoked a day. If Rosko was the first American dj on British radio, 'Fluff' Freeman was surely the first Australian.

It was in Melbourne where he was jocking on a local station that he acquired his nickname. Apparently, it had nothing to do with him fluffing his lines on air but referred to a white sweater which someone had given him and which he wore a lot. After a trip to the dry cleaners it ended up looking like a fluffy sheep. Well, that was his story. In 1957 he left Melbourne for a short sabbatical and never went back. Perhaps, like Rosko, he reasoned that there were more like him back home, but not here.

Like many dj's of the time he started on Radio Luxembourg, graduating to the BBC Light Programme and then Radio One. Along with Jimmy Savile, Pete Murray and David Jacobs, he was one of the original presenters of Top Of The Pops but he made his biggest mark as the presenter of the radio version of the chart show, Pick Of the Pops. With his bouncy theme tune At The Sign Of The Swinging Cymbal by Brian Fahey, he turned the presentation of the chart show into an art form, nipping in between the surges in the music to give the names of the songs and artists and their latest chart position. Many followed him, but none could compare. He also pioneered the idea of inserting clips of classical music into his links. In the early Sixties he starred with Helen Shapiro and Craig Douglas in the film It's Trad Dad (a reference to traditional jazz which was highly popular at the time) and fronted long-running TV campaigns for Brentford Nylons and Omo.

I first met him in 1963. We were booked as joint comperes of a pop show called It's The Geordie Beat for Tyne-Tees TV, recorded at Newcastle City Hall. As I was already in Newcastle, I was despatched to the airport in Ponteland to collect him from a flight from London. I waited and waited and as the last passengers strolled across the tarmac I was convinced he'd missed the plane. Long after the last one had gone, he finally emerged, much to my relief. Obviously, he'd been swamped by the crew who wanted to chat to him and get his autograph. He was a product of the era when there were only a handful of dj's and they were all household names.

When he took over the afternoon show on Radio One in the early Seventies he introduced a feature called 'Get it off your chest' in which listeners were invited to write in about things that really annoyed them. Hundreds of ladies sent him their brassieres which he draped all over the studio – something which is unlikely to happen today.

In 1973 Fluff was quick to leap to the defence of dj's when they were lambasted by newsreader and television presenter Ludovic Kennedy. Speaking to the Royal Society of Arts Kennedy said, "They have no respect for the English language which they constantly mispronounce. They have no vocabulary apart from grunts with which to narrate or describe. They seem wholly contemptuous of what they do not understand which in the case of most of them is a very great deal." Kennedy was critical of the government for banning the pirate stations and said somewhat pompously of the BBC, "What were they going to do? Were they going to deprive millions of the country's more moronic citizens of the sort of fare they so clearly wanted presented in the way they wanted and to which they had got accustomed?"

Fluff hit back: "We keep the population a little happier than Mr. Kennedy does. His deliberations could make half the population feel like committing suicide. When it comes to precise beautiful English, I will challenge him any day he likes. I know some people who speak beautiful English but have the world in a terrible mess." So there.

The Sex Pistols might have finished Bill Grundy's career on Thames TV's Today programme but Fluff was quite happy to take on John Lydon, aka Johnny Rotten, on the revived version of Juke Box Jury with Noel Edmonds. When Johnny started criticising a record by The Monks, Fluff pointed out that the Sex Pistols had sounded like them four years ago. As Rotten continued to rant, Fluff firmly told him to 'shut up'.

With his boxer's face, Alan Freeman looked very butch and few would have guessed that he was gay. One fellow dj who found out was Keith Butler. Keith told me that when he was in his twenties Fluff invited him round to his flat in Maida Vale. After a glass of wine or two Fluff became very flirtatious and more than a little suggestive. Keith kept talking about his girlfriend until finally the penny dropped. Whatever his proclivities, Fluff was very discreet and nothing ever came out.

Fluff Freeman's career at the microphone lasted over fifty years, taking in both the BBC and Capital Radio. He was rewarded with the MBE for services to broadcasting in 1998 and a lifetime achievement award at the Sony Radio Academy Awards in 2000.

He gave up broadcasting in his seventies when he succumbed to a long illness, finishing up for some years in Brinsworth House, the home for ageing actors, in Twickenham. The last time I saw him was at an awards ceremony early in the 2000s. "Do yourself a favour, old love," he said. "Don't ever get old." "We don't have a lot of choice on that one, Fluff," I said. He died in 2006 at the age of 79.

It was sad to see him deteriorate as he did. I prefer to remember him with that big smile, the throaty laugh and that big extrovert personality he had.

Alan Fluff Freeman, one of the all-time great dj's. Not 'arf!

Chapter 9

FIRST LADY OF RADIO ONE

The 'play list' committee that decided which records would, or would not, be played on Radio One was a powerful body, much wooed by song pluggers employed by record companies to get their discs played on the biggest radio station in the UK. It met once a week at Egton House, Radio One's headquarters next door to Broadcasting House, and was chaired by Doreen Davies. At Egton House the BBC had an 'open doors' policy where the pluggers could drop in their latest discs in the hope of getting them played. An airing on Radio One could quite likely lead to a Top Twenty hit.

An even bigger coup would be a Record of the Week on the Noel Edmonds/Tony Blackburn/Johnnie Walker/David Hamilton shows. This would ensure the record was played five times a week on the relevant show and often the other dj's gave it their backing too. The record companies gave the pluggers huge expense accounts so they could wine and dine and schmooze producers and dj's.

Two of them – Alan James, known as The Man in Black, and Dave Most, brother of the legendary record producer Mickie Most, founder of RAK Records whose recording stars included Suzi Quatro and Hot Chocolate – infiltrated the Radio One football team which played charity matches around the country. Sharing a post match bath with the dj's, they couldn't get much closer to them than that. Their main priority was the producers at Egton House who, being rather poorly paid, were usually open to the idea of a liquid lunch. One dined so regularly he earned the nickname 'Egton Ronay'.

Doreen Davies was the station's most senior producer and as such had a great deal of say as to which dj's would be employed. (Her husband, Derek Mills, held a similar position at Radio Two.) She referred to the dj's as 'her boys' and believed that their role was that of surrogate husband, coming into the house via the radio and providing the housewives with the kind of music and chat they wanted during the daytime while hubby was out at work. Women at home made up most of the available audience and there was a strongly held belief at the BBC that they didn't want to listen to other women. The pirates were all men and in the Sixties dj-ing was entirely a male occupation. That being so, it's not surprising there were no women dj's in Radio One's enormous original line-up and listeners had to wait until New Year's Day in 1970 to hear the first female voice when Anne Nightingale launched a Sunday evening show. Ironically, she would outlast all the male dj's and by 2017 had clocked up a remarkable 47 years at the station.

Like John Peel, most of her broadcasting was in the evening and, as with Peel, she discovered new bands rather than churning out chart hits, and played to what was mainly a student audience. Those of us on during the day didn't see a great deal of her, but I worked with her when we co-hosted the notorious Radio One Roadshow from Mallory Park when the Bay City Rollers hopped into a boat on a lake to escape their female fans who jumped in fully clothed and swam after them. Tony Blackburn, oblivious to the whole episode, was swanning around on his jet-ski. It was at the same event that Binkie Baker, Annie's husband, poured a port and brandy over Tony's head after Blackburn had said to him, "Do you mind? We're trying to have a conversation here." Baker later recorded the song Toe Knee Black Burn which ended with the line 'Burn Tony Black'. No pisstake, of course.

The last time I saw Annie was in 2009 and again there was a Blackburn connection. She, Tony and I were guests on the Richard and Judy Show talking about the newly released film The Boat That Rocked, loosely based on the story of Britain's pirate radio days. Tony was booked as an ex-pirate, though he hated the film and said it was full of inaccuracies such as the fact that there were women aboard the ships. Annie was booked as a fan of the pirates and I was there as somebody already working for BBC radio when the pirates were launched. She tottered in on a pair of high heels wearing the blue tinted specs she's sported ever since a terrifying mugging in China which left her on crutches for six months. "I'm still doing lots of gigs, playing to live audiences," she told us, and I thought how brave that was, bearing in mind that she looked so wobbly.

With her journalistic background – she started out as a reporter, then film critic and music reviewer on the Brighton Argus – and her genuine love of music, Annie has indeed been a radio pioneer. Whereas she was for a long time the only female voice on Radio One, she paved the way for many who would follow in her wake like Janice Long, Zoe Ball, Edith Bowman, Jo Wiley and Sara Cox. Today there are more female voices on Radio One than ever before. And while Annie is still there, most of the 'surrogate husbands' are working in commercial radio or in the great disco in the sky.

I had dinner with her one evening at an Indian restaurant in Barnes opposite the Olympic Studios where Procul Harum recorded their Sixties classic A Whiter Shade Of Pale, where The Who cut their album Who Are You? and Jimi Hendrix recorded Are You Experienced? It was clear that the waiters knew her well and it transpired that on a previous visit when her dining companion was Eric Clapton, one of them asked her, "Who's your friend? Is he also in the music business?" Ah, the power of Radio One.

Chapter 10

FROM THE PERFUMED GARDEN

When John Peel presented The Perfumed Garden on Radio London it was obvious that he was going to be different from the other dj's. And so it proved to be. While the likes of Edmonds, Blackburn, DLT and the others were churning out the chart hits during the day on Radio One, Peel was playing the underground and progressive at night to a smaller, though probably more appreciative audience, many of whom were students. The Peel Sessions recorded in BBC studios were the perfect solution to the BBC's 'needle time' problems and sat much more comfortably on his programmes than they did in the daytime.

Peel became a dj almost by accident. Born John Ravenscroft on the Wirral near Liverpool he moved to the USA at the age of 21, working for a cotton producer who'd had dealings with his father. After a series of jobs including travelling insurance salesman, he started doing radio shows for a station in Dallas, moving on to a breakfast show in California, calling himself John Ravencroft. While in America he married 15-year-old Shirley Ann Milburn. When he brought her to England the marriage soon broke up but on the plus side he found a job that would lead to a lifelong career. He landed a show on the pirate station, Radio London, and it was someone there who decided he should change his name to John Peel. His midnight to 2am show brought him more mail than any other jock on the station.

Radio One snapped him up at its launch in 1967 and gave him a programme called Top Gear. Peel said later, "Radio One had no real idea what they were doing. They took people off the pirate ships because there wasn't anybody else." He was a great champion of new bands, but lost interest in them when they became commercial and mainstream. He discovered and promoted Marc Bolan's band Tyrannosaurus Rex, though when they became T Rex and recorded Hot Love and Metal Guru he handed them over to the daytime shows. Those of us who were on during the day saw him rarely. He didn't take part in Radio One roadshows or other team exercises, only appearing at photo calls and Radio One football matches. A lifetime Liverpool fan, he was a keen player and of the entire team he and I were the only ones who were remotely interested in football.

Over time he developed a hatred of Tony Blackburn referring to him as 'Timmy Bannockburn' and the 'anti Christ'. They didn't know each other well so his dislike was probably based mainly on what he thought Blackburn stood for – light entertainment and showbiz, Seaside Special and pantomime, and his projection of himself rather than the music. In fairness to Blackburn, he was interested in the music he played, a great lover of soul and Motown.

Blackburn, in turn, was no fan of Peel, regarding him as having a 'specialist' audience tucked away at off-peak time and that he did nothing for black artists. He also claimed from time to time that Peel didn't actually like much of the music he played, referring to it as 'garbage'. Though John thought Tony was a 'commercial' figure, he was not averse to doing voice-overs on ads. At one stage his voice was heard regularly on several different products. None of this dislike stopped him posing happily in a bath at Fulham Football Club with Tony and me to promote a Radio One match. I didn't detect any bad vibes that day.

Peel also developed a dislike of Simon Bates, though he'd got on with him at first when Bates was a newsreader. He once said after a fancy dress party, "I was going to go as Simon Bates but I couldn't find anybody to wear the other face." Following a Radio One Christmas party, which Peel described as 'the most appalling event of the year', he said, "Kid Jensen, Paul Burnett and I – not a carefully honed fighting team but nevertheless fuelled with drink – waited in the underground car park at the BBC to beat up Bates." Quite what brought this about I don't know, but according to Radio One controller Matthew Bannister, "Bates hated Steve Wright because he saw him as a threat. Wright hated Bates for the same reason. And they both hated DLT." Looking back, it makes me wonder if any Radio One dj had a friend in any other.

Peel and his producer John Walters were left alone for many years because Derek Chinnery, the controller from 1973 to 1985, didn't really understand what they were doing. Whereas Chinnery would constantly criticise Blackburn for his daytime show, it's doubtful if he listened in the evenings. His assistant, Teddy Warrick, a man much more in tune with the listening audience, once nudged me in the direction of Chinnery's private record collection at a party at his house. Prominent albums were South Pacific and The Sound Of Music, much more likely to be his nocturnal listening. But Chinnery did once ask Walters if he was playing any punk, about which he had heard bad things. Walters said, "I had to tell him that almost everything we were playing was punk."

I am sure John Peel was better understood at Radio Four where for years he presented the show Home Truths, and where he found his biggest audience. After his death at the age of 65, the BBC announced that the Egton wing in the new Broadcasting House would be re-named the Peel wing in his honour. Today he is regarded as the most innovative and dedicated dj in Radio One's nearly 50-year history and he lasted longer there than any of the original line-up.

His death came from a heart attack while mountaineering in Peru. He really did die at the top.

Chapter 11

THE CHEEKY MILKMAN

Frinton-on-Sea is a genteel town on the coast of Essex, once home to Winston Churchill and Douglas Fairbanks. Unlike its rowdy neighbour Clacton, it resisted a pier with funfairs, a pub, buses and even a fish and chip shop for many years. It's hardly surprising that many people have chosen to retire there. Back in the days when east coast railways were adorned with billboards heralding "Harwich – Gateway to the Continent", a wag scrawled under one "Frinton – Gateway to the incontinent".

With the arrival of Radio Caroline and Radio London moored off the Frinton coast, the town suddenly became hip. And the man who lit it up more than any other was Johnnie Walker. In his 9 to midnight spot on Radio Caroline he introduced 'Kiss in the Car' and 'Frinton Flashing', which sounded worse than it was, a reference more to motor cars than human beings. Couples would come along in their droves and park on the seafront with their headlights on, pointed at the ship, and then Johnnie would mention them on the air. Rarely has anything personified so perfectly the magic of radio's relationship with its listeners.

Johnnie loved his time on the pirates. He once admitted, "Sometimes women did come aboard. The less attractive ones were given a tour of the transmitter and the generators. The prettier ones would be given another tour." There is a story that did the rounds that Johnnie made the most of one female visitor while on air during Bob Dylan's lengthy classic Like A Rolling Stone, earning him the nickname 'Six-minute Walker'.

While others like Tony Blackburn and John Peel had already departed to the BBC, Johnnie stayed right to the end at Radio Caroline with the result that the BBC took a year to hire him, but by the Seventies he was well established as the lunchtime man on Radio One with his music quiz Pop The Question. With his line of patter he was likened by one journalist to the 'cheeky milkman', as he chatted up the housewives while delivering his daily wares. Like the whiskey that shares his name, he is a strong spirit and has at times been a little wild and headstrong, with the result that his life has been a bit of a rollercoaster ride.

In the Seventies I had established a friendship with Kenny Scott, a down-to-earth cockney who ran the Dun Cow pub in the Old Kent Road (nowadays a dental surgery) and turned it into an entertainment venue. At Sunday lunchtimes he showcased many of the comedians of the day, like Jim Davidson and Mike Reid. I did a disco there for him on Wednesday nights, and he asked if I could get some other Radio One dj's to do it as well. One who agreed was Johnnie Walker, and Johnnie turned up on the agreed night with a bunch of records under his arm with which he intended to entertain the Dun Cow faithful.

Unfortunately, it didn't turn out too well. Whatever the audience reaction was, Johnnie didn't like it. After a few minutes on stage, he picked up his records and said to the crowd, "I've brought some good music along to entertain you lot, but if you can't appreciate it, I'm off," at which point he left not only the stage but also the pub and headed home without his money. Now I've worked to some rough crowds but, having made the effort to get there, I'd have seen it through and made sure I got paid. But, hey, we're all different, and that's how it was for Johnnie.

On another occasion when I invited him along, it turned out to be a memorable evening in a better kind of way, and this time neither of us got paid. One day I had a message at Radio One to contact Keith Cheesman, the chairman of Dunstable Town football club. I knew of him already as he was the man who brought George Best to non-league Dunstable after Bestie had left Manchester United. Keith was getting together a table of guests at Caesar's Palace nightclub near Luton where the American singer Frankie Laine was appearing in cabaret and wondered if I'd like to come along and bring some colleagues from Radio One. I asked around among the gang, and two dj's jumped at it – Johnnie Walker and Emperor Rosko.

It was an Easter Monday, a brilliant evening and I took along as my guest Annie Challis, who was a producer at Radio Luxembourg and always a good laugh. We had the usual 1970s nightclub dinner of scampi in the basket, washed down by plenty of booze and by showtime we were all in a jolly mood. Caesar's Palace's resident compere, Jerry Brooke, came out on stage looking the part in a Roman toga with a laurel leaf in his hair. After a bit of banter he invited 'Our special guests, the Radio One dj's' up on stage. Rosko declined to go but Johnnie and I did, and standing behind Jerry as he did his patter Johnnie leaned across to me and said in my ear, "Let's undo his toga."

"Do you think so?" I said.

"Got to be done," said Johnnie.

With that we both got down on one knee, each holding an end of the cord of his toga. The audience were chuckling. "Right, on three we pull," said Johnnie. I had a split second to decide – would he or wouldn't he? Knowing Johnnie, I reckoned he would. "One, two, three…" he said. We both pulled, and Jerry's toga fell open. The audience roared. Fair play to Jerry – no Y-fronts for him, he was wearing brown matching baggy pants.

Jerry was still chatting away on his hand mike when Johnnie sidled across to me. "The pants have got to go," he said.

"Do you think so?" I stuttered.

"Definitely."

Back down on one knee we went, this time each clutching a leg of Jerry's underpants.

"On three," said Johnnie.

The audience were all falling about, and again I had just a few moments to decide whether Johnnie would do it or not. If I did and he didn't, I'd be the one who went too far. If he did and I didn't, I'd be the one who was chicken. Very quickly I calculated that, knowing Johnnie, he'd do it.

On the word 'three' we both pulled, down came the pants and there was Jerry, still holding the microphone, wearing nothing but an open toga in front of a thousand clubbers at Caesar's Palace. The place was in uproar.

"Ladies and gentlemen, I'm a very modest man," said Jerry, "but then I have a great deal to be modest about."

"No, no," cried the audience.

As we went back to our table, I suddenly sobered up. "Did we go too far?" I asked Annie, my guest. (A stupid question in retrospect.) "If you ever planned it or did it again, it wouldn't work," she said. "But tonight everyone loved it."

The following day Johnnie was handing over to me on Radio One at 2 o'clock. "I'd like to thank you for roping me into a fantastic night at Caesar's Palace in Luton last night and to thank the compere Jerry Brooke for being such a good sport."

"Yes, it was good to see more of Jerry, wasn't it?" I said.

"It certainly was. I think you should play a record for him as a thank-you. Why don't you dedicate your first record to him?"

With that I played the record – and we hadn't planned this – Tie A Yellow Ribbon Round The Old Oak Tree.

A few years later I was back at Caesar's Palace, this time to see Cilla Black in cabaret. One of my dinner companions was the great Bob Monkhouse, my all-time comedy hero. I told Bob the story of the night with Johnnie and, like the title of his autobiography, he was Crying with Laughter. Then a voice-over announced "Please welcome your host – Jerry Brooke." Out came Jerry resplendent in Roman toga. His play-on music was what he later told me had been his signature tune ever since the night I was there with Johnnie… Tie A Yellow Ribbon Round The Old Oak Tree.

That story tells you everything about Johnnie – a fun guy always up for a laugh. Unlike some of the other jocks who saw radio as a route into television, he was a true radio man who loved his music. But just a year after our cover picture, Johnny was on his way out of Radio One, and all because of the Bay City Rollers.

In those days the singles chart came out on Tuesdays and was announced in the last hour of Johnny's show. The Rollers had just had two number ones and so Johnnie had to play them, but he regarded them as 'musical garbage' and was reluctant to do so. Whatever his opinion, the fact was that more people had bought their records than anyone else's at the time and Radio One was the station that played the popular hits. You could say it was a form of musical snobbery but Johnnie was true to his principles and didn't play them. He left to work for a station in San Francisco where he stayed for some time until he discovered, one suspects, that they had a play list he had to stick to as well.

On Johnnie's return to the UK, Ralph Bernard, a long-time admirer of Walker, signed him up for his GWR station (its name inspired by the railway network) covering Swindon, Bristol and Bath. There was a brief return to Radio One before he joined BBC GLR (Greater London Radio). There he stayed until Matthew Bannister – later to become controller of Radio One – sacked him for saying people would be dancing in the streets after Margaret Thatcher resigned as Prime Minister. Like Pete Murray and Kenny Everett, he discovered that spouting controversial words about politics and aligning oneself with a particular party went down badly with the radio hierarchy.

Despite this setback, he was back at Radio One in 1991 and stayed there for four years before moving on to LBC and the Classic Gold network. His intro to Radio Two came via presenting documentary programmes and standing in for other people. One of those he deputised for was John Dunn, a much loved and well respected presenter who'd hosted the afternoon show for many years. But Radio Two was changing and the bosses of the day felt that Walker better fitted the style and image they wanted. When Dunn was let go and replaced by Walker, the BBC was bombarded with complaints from the veteran's loyal band of listeners but, as always in these cases, in time the furore died out, the listeners accepted the change and John Dunn headed off into retirement. A year later Johnnie left the show after an exposé in a Sunday newspaper accused him of using dodgy substances and mixing with undesirables. In the old days at the BBC this would have been a career ender, but Johnnie took himself off to Eric Clapton's rehab in Antigua and got himself clean. Remarkably, the BBC took him back. All was going well until in 2003 he told listeners he was battling cancer and was taking time off for treatment. A year later he was back but, in the true tradition of how radio works, early in 2006 he was replaced on the afternoon show by Chris Evans. Bearing in mind everything he had been through and the following he had built up, this went down with listeners as well as when he took over from John Dunn, but once again in time all the complaints subsided. The one thing programme controllers know is that, no matter how popular someone is, if you take them off the air, in time people will forget. (See next chapter, King of the Togs.)

Since leaving afternoons Johnnie has had a regular Sunday afternoon slot, stood in for Terry Wogan on breakfast for some time, presented a series about the pirates (he was also an adviser on the film The Boat That Rocked) and conducted lots of interviews with rock stars, many of whom have become his mates. Despite announcing that his wife, Tiggy, is now suffering from cancer, it seems that after a turbulent life Johnnie has at last found his true home and a peaceful conclusion to a long and successful career. A lifetime playing the music he loves. Not a bad gig, is it? Better than being a milkman.

Chapter 12

KING OF THE TOGS

Terry Wogan had to thank a BBC producer called Tony Luke for giving him his big break. Luke, who died shortly before Wogan in 2015, was the producer of Late Night Extra, one of the programmes broadcast on both Radio One and Radio Two, in the 10pm to midnight slot when the stations were launched in 1967. Emanating from the production offices of Radio Two, it was more than just a record show, with news, interviews and features as well as music recorded in BBC studios.

Late Night Extra ran successfully for several years, hosted each weekday evening by a different presenter. Tony Luke, who became LNE's executive producer, told me, "The gramophone department were pushing for us to use a young broadcaster from Ireland who'd been tried out on Midday Spin. Unlike so many of the starting line-up, he wasn't an ex-pirate but had begun his career on RTE in Ireland – his name was Terry Wogan. Before we decided to use him, he had to pass an audition, probably the only one he did in his career. He became the Wednesday night man, hosting his first show on 18 October 1967, for which he was paid £33. As he had to travel over from Ireland, the BBC also paid his travel expenses and overnight accommodation. His total fee was £67 3s 6d in old money."

From little acorns...

Terry got his break on Late Night Extra and, after sitting in on Jimmy Young's morning show on Radio One in 1969, he was offered his own daily show from 3 to 5pm. Though he stayed there a while, it was clear that his natural home was Radio Two, and where else would they put their main man than on the breakfast show? There Terry delivered Radio Two an enormous audience in two lengthy spells, either side of hosting his chat show, Wogan, on BBC TV. He was a radio man who moved effortlessly into television but it was on the breakfast show that he built up a cult following, first with 'Fight the Flab' (Bob Monkhouse once quipped, "the flab won") and then with his TOGS, Terry's Old Geezers.

He tore up the rules of broadcasting and invented a style all his own. Dead air with no one speaking – so what? Pacey presentation? Forget it. And how clever was it to get listeners do the work for him with their witty letters and emails, and then sell them back to them in book form!

Millions tuned in every day for Terry's handover with Jimmy Young. Though they bounced off each other well, giving the impression they were great pals, to my knowledge they never socialised as JY was probably as close to being a recluse as anyone in the entertainment business. Terry, one suspected, couldn't wait to get home to the lovely Helen at Wogan Towers in the Thames Valley far from the showbiz hustle and bustle.

With his innate blarney and gift of the gab, he could be very persuasive, and I remember him talking me into turning out in a charity cricket match he was organising at Taplow, though I hadn't played the game for over 20 years.

"If Isla St Clair can play, you can play," he said, and there was no answer to that.

Ernie Wise, Pete Murray, Roy Castle and I were among those who donned the whites for Wogan in what turned out to be a very pleasant afternoon at his local cricket ground. I even managed to score a few runs before Pete Murray, at the other end of the wicket, shouted, "Who do you think you are? Geoffrey Boycott? Throw the bat." So next ball I threw the bat, and was bowled out. Thanks Pete!

But who scored the most runs and hit the winning boundary? Who else but our friend Terry. It couldn't have been stage managed better – a perfect end to a perfect day. I do remember I agreed to play in his cricket match if he'd turn out in a match for the Showbiz XI football team. Surprisingly, that never materialised.

Always in press interviews Wogan would emphasise how lazy he was and not really ambitious. But, hang on a minute, this was the man who in his seventies was still driven enough to get up every morning at the crack of dawn to host a two-hour breakfast show, to present TV shows for various channels, to appear on commercials, write books – and who was shrewd enough to have his own agency that handled the likes of Kenny Everett, Gloria Hunniford and Tony Blackburn, thus not only eliminating the need to pay commission to an agent but also having other artists pay commission to him. At one time he even had a car company with a contract to ferry performers to and from BBC studios. Lazy? I don't think so – but a nice man with it.

I always enjoyed being a panellist when he was hosting Blankety Blank. Unlike other television shows, nothing was ever planned beforehand. It was all ad-lib and good natured fun. It pulled big audiences and remember there were no big prizes. Winners went home with what today would be considered a booby prize – a Blankety Blank cheque book and pen. Blankety Blank had a simple format, it was constantly in the TV Top Ten and its appeal revolved around Terry's light-hearted approach and his banter with the panel.

Even at the height of his success he was easy going and friendly – no 'big time Charlie' like one or two of his colleagues.

He was also able to laugh at himself. There was one day I remember when the Radio Two disc-jockeys were asked to line up for a Radio Times front cover photocall. Along with Terry there was Ken Bruce, Pete Murray, Brian Matthew and myself. The photographer was doing an aerial shot with all of us sitting on a mat in the shape of a 2, as in Radio 2. So as not to make a mark on the mat, he asked us to take our shoes off. When we all dutifully obliged, Terry, of all people, had holes in his socks. All that money and socks with holes in them! We all fell about, and Terry laughed loudest of all. You can imagine the gags on the radio the next day. Terry Wogan, a very religious man – he has holy socks!

Terry received his knighthood in 2005, just three years after his old sparring partner Jimmy Young got his. How strange that only months after becoming Sir Jimmy Young, JY would be dropped from his daily show on Radio Two and replaced by a younger man, Jeremy Vine. Jimmy was offered a weekend show but turned it down, a shame because he could have carried on broadcasting much longer. Having seen what happened to Jimmy, Wogan didn't make the same mistake. When he left the breakfast show he accepted a Sunday show which ran successfully until he was taken ill.

There was an enormous hue and cry when Terry was removed from the daily show, particularly from his loyal army of TOGS who said things would never be the same without him. That was true, but after an initial dip in the audience, it wasn't long before his successor, Chris Evans, was claiming something the BBC never thought possible – even bigger listening figures. Not only that, but probably what Radio Two bosses wanted – younger ones, too. Out with the Old Gits, in with the Young Turks.

Terry deserved his lie-in in the morning. Why would he worry? He had been a unique and charismatic talent on radio and television for over 50 years. All that work plus his business ventures would have made life at Wogan Towers very comfortable indeed. As well as giving Chris Evans his breakfast show, he handed Blankety Blank to Les Dawson and his annual mickey-take on the Eurovision Song Contest to Graham Norton. In time, of course, everything changes and bizarrely the office that once housed his agency in the New Kings Road is now a shop selling rugs.

Until his absence towards the end of 2015 Terry remained an important part of the Radio Two schedule and continued to host Children in Need for BBC TV, as he had done for 34 years. He was also in a position to pick and choose which TV shows he wanted to guest on.

And, unlike some of his colleagues in radio, his life was scandal free.

The other day I was browsing through some old copies of Soccer Star, the national magazine I wrote a column for while still a teenager, when I came across this little gem in the Swap Shop column published on 7 August 1954:

Terence Wogan, 18 Elm Park, Ennis road, Limerick, Eire, has boxing and wrestling magazines, World Sports, Football Monthlies, Sport Magazine, Soccer Stars for any first or second division programmes. Three programmes per boxing and wrestling, World Sport, Football Monthly, two per Sport and Soccer Stars.

Note the businessman in there, and just four days after his 16th birthday. But boxing and wrestling? Terry, you old dark horse.

Could it be another man? I think not. Because as we all know, there was only one Terry Wogan

Chapter 13

THE MAN WHO STARTED IT ALL

When Tony Blackburn launched Radio One at 7am on 30 September 1967 he wrote himself a contract for life. Every time there's an anniversary out comes that clip of him (actually recorded in advance) opening the station under the watchful eye of the Radio One controller, Robin Scott, and introducing the first record played on Radio One, Flowers In The Rain by The Move.

He was the obvious man for the job. A clean cut, good looking ex-public schoolboy with a nice speaking voice and a good set of shiny white teeth, he was radio's equivalent to Cliff Richard. Actually, he was a former singer, having started out in his home town, Bournemouth, fronting Tony Blackburn and The Rovers. Quick to see the potential of the host of the much publicised breakfast show, Harold Davison signed him to his agency. Davison was well connected, the British agent for Frank Sinatra and married to Fifties pop singer Marion Ryan, whose twin boys Paul and Barry had a number of chart hits in the 1960s. Barry Ryan hit number 2 with Eloise in 1968, aided no doubt by plenty of plays on Radio One.

Davison set about launching Blackburn's singing career to broaden his appeal and he had two small hits, So Much Love and It's Only Love in 1968 and 1969. Perhaps the biggest coup was featuring him on one side of an album when on the other side was the man generally regarded as the finest ballad singer of the day, Matt Monro, the former London bus driver who Sinatra called his favourite singer. Some of Monro's early records had been produced by The Beatles' recording manager George Martin who called Matt 'The man with the golden voice'.

Within no time Tony joined the team of hosts of Top Of The Pops and was given his own pop show on Southern TV, Time For Blackburn, though it was obvious he was not as at ease on television as he was on radio where he had learned his trade on the pirate stations. He was a brilliant operator in the studio, very clever in his use of jingles and, of course, there were the corny jokes for which he was famous.

"Did you hear about the butcher who backed into a bacon slicer and got a little behind in his orders?"

When he was younger he was a little naive. He once cracked a joke on air: "Did you hear about the two gnomes who went to a goblin party?" The technical operator next door looked aghast. "Do you realise what you just said?" "Well, I heard it at a party," said Tony. "Everybody laughed and I thought it must be funny, so I wrote it down."

Tony enjoyed six glorious years as the breakfast show host on Radio One. With no breakfast TV or other radio stations to rival it, it's fair to say that everyone who wanted to wake up to music in the morning listened to Tony Blackburn and his barking dog, Arnold, and to a nation that had been starved of pop music, apart from the short but spectacular run of the pirates, this was just what they needed. For those who were angry about the axing of the pirates, here was one of their boys leading the team.

Tony himself enjoyed a high profile in magazines like Jackie and Mirabelle and was often seen out on the town with the glamorous model, Lyn Partington. After their affair fizzled out he met and married the actress Tessa Wyatt. Here was a showbiz marriage made in heaven – the good looking young dj and the pretty young actress. When their son, Simon, came along everything in the Blackburn household was perfect, including the house with swimming pool they bought at Cookham near the River Thames. It was here that things started to go wrong.

Among their neighbours at Cookham were Roger Webb, the songwriter and producer, and his wife Margo. Suffice it to say, they became a little too neighbourly which led to the break-up of both marriages. Later Tessa got together with Richard O'Sullivan, her co-star in the series Robin's Nest. Though they had a son, they never married. Richard took early retirement from show business and became probably the youngest actor at Brinsworth House, the residential home for entertainers. Tessa went on to marry someone else. 'Magnificent Margo', as Tony called her in his second autobiography, eventually re-united with Roger, mourning his death at the age of 68.

The hiatus in his marriage caused Tony problems at Radio One. Derek Chinnery, the controller, was so fond of him that Tony was often referred to as 'the son Derek never had'. After most shows they would have breakfast together in the BBC canteen.

One thing Derek encouraged him to do was talk about his family on air. This was fine until things went wrong in his marriage and Tony started sending on-air messages to Tessa begging her to come back and playing Gary Benson's record Don't Throw It All Away. As Tony said at the time, he couldn't talk about something on-air one minute and then suddenly brush it under the carpet, but his outpourings were bringing a sad tone to his programmes. Chinnery had already moved Tony from the breakfast show and replaced him with the younger Noel Edmonds. Blackburn took this badly and there is in existence a tape of a handover between Noel and him that is so frosty you can almost see the icicles in the studio. Now Chinnery was becoming critical of his broadcasts, which added to Tony's feelings of gloom.

I'd been friendly with Tony since the early days of Radio One. When we became the first dj's to have three-hour programmes (Tony in the morning, and me in the afternoon) we decided to be rude about each other on our shows, a way of publicising each other's programmes while leaving the audience to speculate on whether we really disliked each other or if it was part of a long-running gag. It meant tapping in to a large repertoire of 'insult' jokes.

"There's nothing I wouldn't do for him, and nothing he wouldn't do for me. And that's how we go through life - doing nothing for each other."

"Tony Blackburn's very upset because somebody broke into his private library and stole both his books. One of them he hadn't finished colouring in yet."

He appeared on an edition of Top Of The Pops wearing a T-shirt saying 'I Hate David Hamilton'. As well as Top Of The Pops, BBC TV had signed us up as presenters of Seaside Special, the summer series that was transmitted on Saturday nights under a circus tent in seaside resorts around the UK. In the early days Tessa and my girlfriend Kathy McKinnon came along.

Kathy and I followed Tony and Tessa on a holiday to Barbados. We arrived on the day they were leaving and overlapped for just a few hours. It was pretty clear that things had not been going well. Tessa talked to Kathy and I talked to Tony but I didn't hear them speak to each other. Soon after, Tessa left Tony. Naturally, he was very down and hit an all-time low and, as friends do at such times, I did my best to cheer him up. I told him he had a lot of good things going for him – he was young, good looking, had a good career and money in his pocket and that in time he would meet someone else. He took a bit of convincing but a while later when my relationship with Kathy broke up, I said to him, "Look, there are lots of great women out there. Let's go out and meet them". His other good friend was Phil Swern, then a record producer. In our different ways we got him through.

Back then he didn't seem to have much idea about money or how to invest it. He didn't appear to have any idea how much he was earning and left everything to an accountant. I told him he should get a government bond that, ironically, was called a TESSA. He did and having lost one Tessa, he gained another. We spent a lot of evenings at a restaurant near where I lived in Barnes run by a cockney/Italian called Umberto, known to his friends as Bert, who said 'Innit?' after everything. As in "What would you like to drink, innit?" When Bert decided to move on we loved the restaurant so much we thought of buying it. It's just as well we didn't because Tony, a lifetime vegetarian, has little interest in food. Imagine a restaurant run by a man whose favourite meal is omelette and chips and a business partner whose culinary skills run to boiling eggs and baking jacket potatoes.

We had fun times there and lots of other places, too, and I do believe I helped him get over the trauma of his broken marriage. After being Radio One's golden boy, he was now on the slide. Four and a half years after moving him from the breakfast to the morning show, Derek Chinnery shunted him off to afternoons and not much later off a daily show and on to Junior Choice, the kids' request show at weekends. Ultimately, Tony sought solace at BBC Radio London where his 'sex and soul' show became cult listening among London's taxi drivers with Tony, the master of double entendre, talking about his 'twelve incher'.

In 1988 things were changing at Capital Radio. Like Radio One, the station had originally begun broadcasting on AM (medium wave), in Capital's case on 1548 metres. By the late Eighties it was heard on the much superior FM signal, and the Radio Authority decreed that it must provide an alternative service on 1548 or give up the wavelength to another station. The decision was made at Capital Towers that 1548 would be a 'Gold' service, providing listeners with 24 hours of golden oldies. Blackburn was hired as the breakfast jock, followed by me with a three-hour morning show, Paul Burnett with a lunchtime chart show, Kenny Everett in the afternoon and Graham Dene at 'drive time'. Overnight and weekend jocks included the big American with the big voice, Randall Lee Rose, Dave Cash (who sounded American) and record producer and dj Stuart Coleman, who did a rock 'n' roll show. It was the 'dream team' and the station opened with a blaze of publicity and started off like an express train.

Despite its dodgy signal which disappeared in tunnels and other locations, at certain times of the day it had more listeners than the FM station. In time we realised this was not what Capital wanted. The people who sold the advertising were more interested in the flagship FM station which was playing to the younger listeners, and its biggest rival, poaching its audience, was right here in the same building. Which is why after a while Blackburn discovered Chris Tarrant on the FM breakfast show was giving away anything up to £100,000 while he was giving listeners Capital Gold pens. All this presented a dilemma for Capital's programme controller, Richard Park. An ex-pirate dj on Radio Scotland and former host of 'Doctor Dick's Midnight Surgery' on Radio Clyde, he was a man who liked his football analogies. As controller of both Capital FM and Capital Gold, he was like the manager of two football clubs – one that he wanted to win the league, and one he wanted to come second. It was an impossible task and in time the Capital Gold team split up. Graham Dene was the first to go, replaced by Mike Read. Kenny Everett left due to ill health in 1994. A year later he died at the tragically young age of 50, an enormous loss to the broadcasting industry. For us all it was a very sad time. Blackburn was the last to go, moving on to another oldies station, Classic Gold, which broadcast from a converted school in Dunstable, a far cry from his days at Broadcasting House.

It was while he was working for Capital Gold that Tony met the girl who would become his second wife, the dancer and actress Debbie Thomson, and I was their best man when they got married in 1990. My six years at Capital Gold brought Tony and me back together again. Taxi drivers, in particular, seemed to love our daily 'handover' where Tony dubbed us the 'Twin Peaks', based on the TV series at the time, and where we were back to swapping 'insult gags'. Tony referred to himself as Mr Magic and me as Mr Tragic, though when I called him Mr Plastic he seemed to go off the idea a bit. Lots of offers came in to do our double act at discos and clubs and, although Capital Gold was heard only in London, we travelled all over the UK to appear on stage in our gold suits, Tony with his huge medallion which he liked to swing round his head, calling it his Big Whopper. Paul Burnett, a man with a dry sense of humour, described us as the best double act since Burke and Hare, though he did add, "but they both want to be the Hare."

Tony said it was nice to have company on the road instead of travelling on his own but I can't say that working with him was easy. Before we went on stage he would often put the management through the wringer. At one venue he said he wouldn't go on because the stage was too small for him to dance around on. The manager apologised profusely but said at that late time he wouldn't be able to get hold of a bigger stage. I knew Tony would appear because I knew he wouldn't go home without the money. Eventually, of course, he did appear. Result – a very grateful and relieved manager.

At a corporate Christmas event in London the organisers told us their chairman planned to make a speech while we were on. Tony said it wasn't a good idea because he and I had an act and it would destroy the flow of our act. The chairman who, after all, was paying our wages was adamant that he wanted to go on and after what seemed like an hour of negotiations Tony reluctantly agreed. As it turned out, the chairman's speech was the highlight of the evening and if anything enhanced our show.

One night we were booked at a club in Surrey. I was doing a radio show in London and Tony agreed to go on first and that I would join him as soon as I could get there. When I arrived the manager showed me into the dressing room and asked if I would like some champagne to give away to the best dancers. I immediately snapped up his invitation. He said he'd offered some to Tony but Tony said, "No, give them to David. I've got an act."

When we were working in Bournemouth his mother invited us to dinner before the show. We had such a lovely evening with his mother and his sister, Jackie, that it seemed a shame to spoil it by going to work. As we were about to leave and Tony went to the loo, his mother said something quite revealing to me: "Look after him, won't you?" "I always have," I said. I wonder if she knew that Tony called me the brother he never had, though he always added, "But I never wanted a brother anyway." I did have to look after him. Most of the time I did the driving. In the small hours of the morning we were almost back in London from a gig in Northampton when he discovered he'd left something at the club so we had to head back up the M1 and collect it. Another night I drove him to hospital and stayed with him in A & E after he fell off a stage and broke his wrist.

On our disco tour we started playing universities. We were apprehensive about this at first because we didn't quite know what young audiences would make of a couple of old boys in gold lamé suits. At Sheffield we followed a cool rock band dressed in black, but once we got on stage we found the students not only accepted us but lapped up the vintage music we were playing.

By the late Nineties Tony was disenchanted with his agent and suggested he might approach mine. When I spoke to my agent he was keen on the idea of managing Tony and said it could be good for both of us if we were under the same banner. Though I was enthusiastic about the idea, the agent didn't get us any work together. But an opportunity did come along that sent Tony's career off into orbit.

In 2000, ITV were about to launch a new series called I'm A Celebrity – Get Me Out Of Here. Both his mother and his wife were against him doing it, fearing how he would cope not so much with the spiders and snakes as with the people – and there were some difficult ones. Tony was determined to do it and my hunch was that he would win it. I was even more convinced when I saw he was the only remaining male contestant, and I said so in an interview on the ITN News and in an article in a daily newspaper. I could predict the headline, 'King of the Jungle', and sure enough it happened.

Winning I'm A Celebrity propelled Tony into hosting peak-time TV shows (though this didn't last long) and, of course, every time the show comes back, as the first winner he's invited along to make his comments about the current cast.

Tony's always been known for his pithy comments, but sometimes they've come back to haunt him. At his 60th birthday party at the Chesterfield Hotel in London he asked me to make a speech and I did so in the spirit of the insult jokes we'd always enjoyed. I mentioned his quote about sleeping with 250 women and said I'd told him that saying that was not a good career move. When he asked me why, I said, "Only 250? A few days afterwards Kenny Lynch said he'd slept with 5,000." A couple of years later when Tony mentioned the subject again, the total he quoted had risen to 500.

In another quote he said he'd never read a book. This rang true when he was a subject of Piers Morgan's Life Stories in 2014 and it quickly became apparent that Piers was more familiar with Tony's second autobiography, Poptastic, than the man himself. On the programme Tony admitted that the book, which succeeded in upsetting quite a number of people, had been written not by him but by Cheryl Gansey, a former producer at BBC Radio London. Tony wouldn't be the first person to have his autobiography ghosted by someone else, but in his case what was remarkable was that he hadn't even read it before it went to the printers. One of the people upset by the book was his wife Debbie who has, one suspects, been quite a steadying influence in his life. After they married she gave up performing and became an agent. With her understanding of the business she has, I'm sure, impressed on him the importance of making contacts and being polite to the right people.

In 2014 I was one of the people who paid tribute to him on the anniversary of his 50 years in radio. We swapped insult gags as usual, and I know he wouldn't expect anything different in this book.

In one of his best quotes he said, "I don't have friends because they get in the way of business." It came as quite a shock to those of us who thought we had been friends to him because it made us think that perhaps we'd been wasting our time.

A friend he seemed to have lost track of was Richard Swainson, an ex-pirate dj and best man at his wedding to Tessa Wyatt. In 2015, a BBC South Today programme captured the moment that Swainson turned up at a radio studio much to the surprise of Blackburn who thought he was dead. It was a good publicity story but only Tony would have failed to see the irony in the fact that he had totally lost touch with someone who was once important enough in his life to be his best man.

Outside of radio, Tony doesn't appear to have a lot of interests. He's a lifetime fan of Coronation Street and more than once has dropped the hint that he'd love to appear on it. And he's passionate about his children – Victoria, who looks destined to follow him into the business, and Simon, who's adept at getting him sponsors for his radio shows. But there are some things he hates with a vengeance, and one of them is football. Though he wasn't a bad player in the Radio One football team, he can't stand the game. We were doing a gig on Teeside and Middlesbrough were having a particularly good season. "Any Middlesbrough supporters here?" I said, and the place erupted. "I hate football," said Tony. Brave if nothing else.

He was always touchy about people who took over from him. Apart from the Noel Edmonds incident, there was very bad feeling when Simon Bates took over the morning show, especially as he inherited Tony's Golden Hour and became so synonymous with it. Following a run-in they had in a national newspaper, there was a further spat as we were waiting to go on set at the 25th anniversary edition of Top Of The Pops. The next moment the floor manager was ushering us on to the set and there we were beaming on camera, all good pals, the happy faces of Radio One!

In 2012, with me in my seventies and Tony not far off his, we did a dance routine on Let's Dance For Sport Relief to Salt 'n' Pepper's Push It and the following year we were contestants on Pointless. Unfortunately, we got knocked out in the second round when Tony thought Andorra was a capital and not a country. Ironically, the next round was on Eighties music.

After bumping around in the world of commercial radio and on local stations, it must have been one of the happiest days in his life when, thirty years after leaving Radio One, he finally got the call back to Broadcasting House as the host of Pick Of The Pops. 2016 was a wretched year when the BBC took him off the air after he'd been questioned at an internal inquiry about Jimmy Savile. Less than a year later they took him back and gave him Sounds Of The Sixties and the Golden Hour that he lost so long ago. So he's back where he started and amazingly he's the only one of the twenty-two dj's in that original Radio One photo on the steps of All Souls Church in 1967 who was still broadcasting on national radio 50 years later. Whenever I bump into him, he's quick to tell me and anyone else who cares to listen that these days he's on six different radio stations. I've often thought his ultimate ambition is to have his own station and broadcast on it 24 hours a day.

You have to hand it to the guy. He's been knocked down a few times, but he keeps bouncing back. For 50 years he's remained a household name and he's lost none of his enthusiasm and his love of hard work.

The ultimate survivor.

Chapter 14

THE FIRST NOEL

R adio Luxembourg proved to be a successful hunting ground for the BBC. Starting with Pete Murray in the Fifties, many young broadcasters learned their trade at FAB 208. Following Pete came the likes of Barry Alldis, Paul Burnett, David 'Kid' Jensen, Peter Powell and Noel Edmonds who arrived at Radio One in 1969.

Edmonds' first job was making trailers for forthcoming programmes but he was keen and eager and it wasn't long before he was given his own shows. Being that bit younger than most of the other jocks, he was the obvious choice to take over the breakfast show in June 1973, just four months before legal land-based commercial radio was launched in the UK. Off the air he quickly established himself as an Action Man, flying a helicopter and becoming a racing car driver of some promise.

It all began when some bright spark came up with the idea of Radio One race days at Brands Hatch. Imagine a bunch of incompetent, untrained young men hammering their cars far too fast around a tight race track also occupied by experienced drivers, and you get the picture. Consider, too, that those young men are the stars of your station and that any one of them could be involved in a serious accident and you realise how remarkable the whole thing was. Only Noel showed any talent at the sport and at one time it looked as though he might go on to become a serious racer. It was through the racing at

Brands Hatch that he met Mike Smith. When Smith, inspired by Noel, became a Radio One dj himself, he did have a bad accident at Oulton Park, breaking both his legs.

From the breakfast show Noel's career went into orbit. He joined the rota of hosts of Top Of The Pops and on Saturday mornings his audience of young listeners followed him to Multi Coloured Swap Shop. It ran from 1976 to 1982, at which time BBC TV bosses moved him to the peak-time Saturday night slot with The Late Late Breakfast Show. It was a big move indeed. For many years Saturday night BBC entertainment had been dominated by double acts like Morecambe and Wise, Little and Large and Cannon and Ball; magicians like David Nixon and Paul Daniels; and singers like Val Doonican. Now it was in the hands of a Radio One dj and he made it work, but four years down the line disaster struck. The series was cancelled after Michael Lush plummeted to his death while rehearsing a bungee jump.

Two years later Noel bounced back with his Saturday Roadshow and then in 1991 with Noel's House Party. With its grunge tank, gotchas and Mr. Blobby, it ran on Saturday nights for eight years. One of the regulars on it was Tony Blackburn, though most of his appearances were humiliating and consisted of Noel doing things like slamming the door in his face. Tony took it all in good spirits, though it emphasised the gulf between where their careers had come to – Noel the highly paid host and Tony doing a guest spot for a few quid and having the door slammed in his face. The difference in their lifestyles was probably emphasised even more when Noel invited Tony to his sprawling estate in Devon and flew him over it in his helicopter. How the other half lives!

Noel was among the guests at Tony's 60th birthday party in 2004. Though not invited to speak, he stood up at the end of the evening and paid such a moving tribute to Tony that our host was moved to tears. But the biggest surprise of the night was when Noel's wife, Helen, got to her feet and started saying how she had loved listening to the breakfast show when Tony was doing it and how much better he was than Noel. "That's the end of my marriage," said Noel, who was sitting next to me, and not long after it was. Every career has its hiccups, and this was a bad time for Noel. The House Party had come to an end – with hindsight Noel might have believed he'd done one series too many – and he parted acrimoniously with the BBC. They say when you're down is the time people kick you and, to compound his misery, in 2004 Channel 5 maliciously devised a programme called The Curse Of Noel Edmonds. It was the kind of hatchet job that television does from time to time that shows the vicious side people in the industry can have to their fellow workers. One of the people who took part in it was Mike Read who told me that when they met at a function some time afterwards Noel offered him 'outside'. Mike, a gentle soul, declined the offer which was just as well because on reach alone he would probably have come off better.

If 2004 provided the nadir of his career, Noel was to prove again that 'bouncebackability' was his trump card. His agent, John Miles, had spotted that good new game shows were coming out of the Netherlands and that one in particular looked a real winner. In 2005 he managed to persuade bosses at Channel 4 that Noel was the right man to front a new show called Deal Or No Deal. How right he was. Originally booked for 66 shows, it has run successfully for over ten years. Tune in any afternoon and you could see Noel as the master of his craft, moving effortlessly around the set, charming the contestants, particularly the young ladies, ad-libbing everything without an autocue just as he did on House Party. It was a lucky show for him. It even found him a new wife, make-up artiste Liz Davies, whom he met on the show in 2006.

So life was good again for Noel. As he once said, "I enjoy being me." In a more recent interview he said he was now worth £70 million, not bad going for someone whose divorce from his second wife just ten years before had lost him his country estate and a great deal more. He also said he didn't have friends among the other dj's when he was at Radio One. Friendships were difficult when dj's were rivals fighting over the same scraps that were available, and there was always bad feeling when somebody took over someone else's slot, as though the new incumbent had been guilty of some form of skulduggery. This did happen, of course, but mostly it was the case that people wanted to work, and to get any show they had to wait until another dj was pushed. Noel put his lack of friends at the station down to the fact that "All the other dj's were jealous because I had the breakfast show." Actually, that's not quite right. We were all so busy with our radio and TV shows and our gigs that we didn't have much time to think about what anybody else was doing.

Bearing in mind what an intelligent and innovative broadcaster he was in the Seventies and Eighties, it seems a shame there isn't a slot for him on one of the major radio networks today. Or maybe that's his choice, and he doesn't hanker to return to radio.

He still has plenty to offer to television, but down the years he's had another career. With varying degrees of success, he's been involved in a number of business ventures. Take a closer look at that luxuriant hair and the beard, and you might think his inspiration has been more Richard Branson than Kenny Everett.

Chapter 15

A DIDDY IN THE AFTERNOON

When Derek Chinnery called me into his office at Egton House in the spring of 1973 and told me I was getting my own daily show on Radio One it was something I'd waited for for a long time. I was hardly an overnight success. It came fourteen years after my first radio show, and after years of interviewing pop stars on Radio One Club and standing in for people like Jimmy Young and Terry Wogan. I was 34 and it really was a case of now or never. Actually, at that point I'd done more television than radio, working as a programme host on most of the ITV companies around the country. But unlike those who saw radio as a stepping stone into television, for me it had always been my first love.

As an only child growing up on a remote farm with only our sheepdog for company as we roamed the fields, the radio was my window to the world. It brought in 'the sound of London traffic' in In Town Tonight and the descriptive football commentaries by Raymond Glendenning from places like St James's Park and Old Trafford. I could only imagine huge crowds and what London and Newcastle and Manchester were like – let alone Dunfermline and Stenhousemuir when I heard them on the football results! At Christmas time I 'entertained' the family with my impersonations of the stars of ITMA and Take It From Here. By the time the teenage years had arrived I'd moved on to listening to Radio Luxembourg with its wonderful mix of music. I had two passions, football and music, and two boyhood heroes – Sam Bartram, the Charlton goalkeeper, and Pete Murray, the Luxembourg dj. When I realised I wasn't good enough to make a living playing football, I decided it might be easier to be a disc-jockey. My school mates laughed at me and said, "How are you going to do that with your sarf London accent when all the people on the wireless talk posh?" To find the answer, I hired a huge Grundig tape recorder, lugged it home and read newspaper articles and adverts into it until I rounded off the edges and started to sound like the guys who were on air.

After leaving school my first real job was as a script-writer at ATV, one of the new commercial television stations. Just when the writing job was going well, I was being called up for National Service in the RAF. It was only after pestering a careers officer that I managed to get a posting to Lincolnshire changed to one abroad. While the rest of my squadron went to Digby, I was on a troop ship to Holland and then to RAF Butzweilerhof near Cologne, home of the British Forces Network in Germany (now BFBS). I didn't have a job there, but I got one after a meeting with the station director when I persuaded him that, while the other shows were playing Bing Crosby and Peggy Lee, what the troops wanted was rock 'n' roll and that I was the one to play it. It was an exciting time in Germany because Elvis Presley was there doing his National Service with the US Army.

Returning to the UK in 1960 I found there were virtually no openings in radio but later that year I did land a job as a television announcer in Manchester. Throughout the Sixties I hosted TV shows for stations around the country and did a light entertainment series with Ken Dodd in the middle of the decade which landed me with a new nickname, Diddy. And I worked for the BBC Light Programme on all the various record and tape shows they produced – Swingalong, Swing Into Summer, Roundabout, Music Through Midnight, Midday Spin and Housewives Choice.

Where the pirates were concerned I missed the boat. Why would I leave a wife and two children in Manchester and lots of television work to be tossed about on the high seas? My wife would have thought I was crazy to even suggest it and I never thought the BBC would take the pirates seriously. They were illegal, weren't they? Surely the BBC wouldn't take on people who had been broadcasting illegally? Well, I got that one wrong.

When they did I was devastated not to be in the original Radio One line-up or in that photograph of the guys on the steps of All Souls Church opposite Broadcasting House. It came back in newspapers and magazines again and again. Meanwhile, I was tucked away in the bowels of Broadcasting House playing The Golden Sounds of Frank Chacksfield on Radio Two. I was playing music for people in their seventies and eighties and I wasn't yet in my thirties. I suppose I was synonymous with the old scripted style of the Light Programme.

Some of the pirates didn't last, and after nearly six years of standing in for other people and doing some Radio One Clubs, my time finally came. As if the news of a daily Radio One show wasn't enough, Chinnery told me that, along with Tony Blackburn, I would have the longest ever show on Radio One – three hours. Blackburn would do mornings and I would be on from 2 until 5 in the afternoon. It seemed almost too good to be true – and it was.

A couple of days later Chinnery asked to see me again. This time he told me that a percentage of my programme would be non-needle time – in other words, tapes recorded at BBC studios, either by groups doing cover versions of their own hits or by BBC house orchestras. As the programme launched in June 1973, it became evident to my producer and me that a third of the programme would be on tape and we would have to work round this as best we could. If the listeners rumbled it wasn't a record show, we could lose them in droves. Tapes and cover versions were what everybody hated about the old Light Programme and why they had defected in their droves to the all-record-playing pirates. We were going to have to be masters of disguise. Where groups went into studios and produced something that sounded roughly like the original record we could play it. When their efforts sounded nothing like the original, we played the disc instead. What did it matter? The musicians had been paid, and that was the main issue.

The problem we couldn't get around was the music that was used in a feature called Tea At Three. Following an excellent jingle of Everything Stops For Tea (actually recorded by the band Mud) came a six minute segue of songs by Johnny Arthey's band and singers. No disrespect to Johnny who had worked on many successful records but six minutes of a band and singers covering other artists' hits was an instant turn-off. Sometimes I looked at the number of tapes that were clogging up the show and came to the conclusion that the only way not to play them was for me to talk more – hence endless request messages.

In retrospect, some of the features I was given to do were out of step with a time when the Women's Lib movement was gathering momentum. David Hamilton's Beauty Tips For Women (later the subject of a book) with a man telling women how to make themselves attractive was perhaps not the best idea, especially when preceded by a jingle featuring a clip from the song Keep Young And Beautiful which included the lines...

Keep young and beautiful. It's your duty to be beautiful.
Keep young and beautiful if you want to be loved.
Imagine how that would go down today! Probably even worse than it did in 1973.

Luckily, there were lots of things listeners did like including my daily Music Game where I asked questions about music and a contestant won an album for every correct answer. It brought forth some real music buffs and the best of them would compete in a grand final in the concert hall at Broadcasting House. After all these years I still hear from Alan Jarvie who travelled down from his home in Scotland to win the final.

Another popular feature was Radio One Makes Your Day, where we'd send a bouquet of flowers to a woman celebrating a birthday or wedding anniversary. The flowers would arrive ahead of a phone call from the studio when we'd chat about how she was going to spend her special day. The flowers and the call would come as a surprise to the lady of the day and 'Thank you for the lovely flowers, David' became such a catchphrase that a bunch of hairy rockers greeted me with it at a Doobie Brothers concert at the Rainbow, Finsbury Park. Radio One Makes Your Day was the inspiration for Gerald Harper's Champagne And Roses which followed later at Capital Radio.

Despite the needle-time problems the programme seemed to attract a loyal following. In the 70s and 80s Radio One dj's were so newsworthy that we joked that we only had to fart and it would make headlines. For four years I lived with the model and page 3 girl Kathy McKinnon. Her father was a High Court judge and when he handled a controversial case there would often be references to Kathy and me. After I sold my life story to a Sunday newspaper for the third time, Kathy and I were concerned that an IRA bomb might blow us off the front page so at 1 in the morning we went to Piccadilly Circus to pick up an early edition. Once we saw we were there we went off happily to bed. We turned into publicity junkies and it was a challenge to see how famous we had become. When we went to the premiere of Abba–The Movie we got more coverage than the Swedish quartet. A lot of this hunger for publicity sprang from insecurity. Radio One was constantly dropping dj's and replacing them with younger ones, so doing plenty of television and being newsworthy gave us a high profile and in theory stopped us falling by the wayside.

Two years into my stint at Radio One the BBC, in one of its periodical economy cuts, axed the afternoon show on Radio Two and had the DH Show broadcast simultaneously across both networks. Radio Two in those days had a signal that stretched from Ireland to Paris and the joint audience from the two networks gave me the highest audience of any show during the day. All this led to lots of requests to appear in discos around the country. The money was attractive. In one night at a club we could earn what took a week at Radio One. I turned up at the first one, the Camelot Club in Taunton, with not the slightest idea of what to do. While the records were on, I noticed lots of people staring at me as though they were waiting for something to happen. What were they expecting? Cartwheels? Somersaults? They must have been disappointed.

So I went back and asked the other guys what they did. Someone recommended 'Two in a T-shirt' where you get a woman on stage to model a Radio One T-shirt, then invite a bloke up and discover – surprise, surprise – you've only brought one T-shirt with you so they'll have to share it. That usually got a laugh. Then there was the beer drinking contest. You get four guys up on stage with four female assistants.

When the beer arrives, it's in baby bottles and the girls have to sit on their laps and feed them. Unfortunately, beer appears to be more intoxicating when drunk from a baby bottle, as I discovered when one of the contestants threw up all over the stage.

It's ironical that today dj's are paid a fortune to 'mix' records together without necessarily saying anything. When we were booked at clubs we were expected to put on a show almost like a cabaret act.

One night at a club called Ragamuffins in Camberley a girl in the audience asked if she could dance on stage while I was on. I told her I didn't use dancers on my show. She said, "You will when you've seen me." She told me she was an African princess, and naturally I believed her. Princess Balou looked absolutely sensational as she stripped down to a leopard-skin bikini and once she started gyrating on stage nobody could take their eyes off her. After the show I told her I would use her on some of my gigs and started taking her with me as I toured around the country. As time went by she became bolder and bolder. She'd invite a man up on stage to dance with her and then undress him, starting with his shirt. Usually that was about as far as it went but at a club in Brentwood she removed the rest of his clothing as well. Several women complained and the following Sunday the News of the World ran the headline "Diddy David Disco Dancer Banned". Underneath was a picture of us on stage and some quotes from the club's manager saying that he would never have either of us back in his club again. The following day my agent had a record number of calls from clubs and halls wanting me to appear, but insisting I bring my dancer with me as well.

During my time at Radio One I was doing at least three discos a week and a lot of travelling. One night I'd be in

Aberdeen, the next Plymouth and the one after that Belfast. After a while, as I made more contacts, I got to realise that it made more sense to concentrate a run of gigs in the same area, far apart enough not to clash – say, Liverpool, Manchester and Bolton. The gigs were always late at night and the manager or owner invariably wanted to have a chat before we drove home – fine for him because he lived around the corner, but not so good on the nights we had to drive back to London.

One day I got Judy, my PA, to contact the makers of Disco crisps to see if they would be interested in me throwing out packets of their crisps to the audience. The message came back that they would and a few days later a large lorry pulled up at my flat in Hallam Street, round the corner from the BBC, and two men delivered so many boxes of crisps that every room of the flat was piled high to the ceiling with them. Days later a PR person from the company asked how the crisps were going down with the punters. "They love them," said Judy who was then asked, "How much do we owe you for promoting them?" Judy plucked a figure out of the air, and a few days later a cheque arrived. Next on board were Ricard, who supplied us with drinks, and Leichner who did make-up sessions at the venues I played. By now I was wearing on stage a Ricard hat, a Disco Crisps T-shirt and a Leichner jacket. I was sponsored from head to toe. And the revellers went home well fed, well refreshed and looking good!

Most of the gigs were at weekends but frequently a club would book one of us on a Tuesday night. It was a dead night but they thought a Radio One dj would pack in the crowds. Sometimes it worked. If it was a long way away there was the mad dash back to London the following day to arrive in time for the show. I never missed one. As well as the gigs, there was Top Of The Pops and on Sundays I played football for the Showbiz XI, which kept me fit. On two nights a week I was on screen as an announcer for Thames TV, so I'd finish at Radio One at 5, drop in at my flat in Hallam Street to change and then head to the Thames studios in Euston Road to be on air at 5.45.

Being so busy, my time at Radio One went by in a whirl. Everybody says Sixties music was the best but I reckon the Seventies sounds were great, too. Despite the miners' strikes, the three-day working week and rampant inflation, the Seventies were a fun time. And, of course, there were the two fabulous summers of '75 and '76. On Radio One I was pumping out the summer sounds. It was the Isley Brothers and Summer Breeze and Bobby Goldsboro with Summer (The First Time).

The problem with a programme that spanned two networks was that it was in danger of falling between two stools – being too sharp for Radio Two, as it was then, and too blunt for Radio One. But it soldiered on that way for three years until the BBC found the money to divide the networks again. When that happened it was decided among the hierarchy that I would move to Radio Two. Who would they put up against me on Radio One? Tony Blackburn. A masterpiece of planning. Neither of us thought it was a good idea. I felt it would spell the end of my club appearances, though once the move was made it didn't make a lot of difference.

At Radio Two I worked with a series of good producers, including Geoff Mullin, Chris Vezey and Martin Cox, who made sure the music was sharper than that on any of the other programmes. It was a kind of Radio One-and-a-half which pleased the listeners but not my former colleagues at Radio One. One day my old Radio One producer came storming into the studio while I was on air, shouting, "You're playing our music." No one told me that Radio One had Abba under exclusive contract. Despite great efforts by Derek Chinnery to have any semblance of pop music eradicated from my programme, Geoff Owen, the controller of Radio Two, stood his ground and said, "You worry about your network and I'll worry about mine."

I stayed twice as long as the afternoon man at Radio Two than I did at Radio One. It would have been even longer had it not been for the arrival of a new controller, Frances Line, who set the station back years by introducing a nostalgia package that included 'pan pipes, whistling and Wurlitzers' but not a mention of Motown, probably the greatest nostalgia package of all. One week I was playing T Rex, the next, at her behest, Max Bygraves and Foster and Allen. Listeners complained in droves. I couldn't do it. It was too much of a gear change too quickly. I knew it was wrong for the station and as a matter of principle I had to move on. No one says today that Frances Line took Radio Two in the right direction, nor is the irony lost on me that the Radio Two of today is the one I was advocating then. After 25 years at the BBC, it was time to sample the world of commercial radio. But that's another story.

Chapter 16

BRITAIN'S FIRST NUDE DJ

Dj's loved playing tricks on each other. Setting fire to a script someone was reading (yes, really), dousing a colleague with water, putting a pair of pyjama bottoms over someone's head – all these happened while a broadcaster was talking to the nation in the hope it would make him 'corpse'. Invariably it worked.

David Symonds, one of the original line-up of Radio One, had one of the best voices heard on music radio. A product of the BBC Light Programme, rather than the pirate radio ships, he divided the peak years of his career between the BBC and Capital Radio. By the early Eighties he was hosting Much More Music, the teatime show on Radio Two, where the music suited his own mellow tones. But Symonds was something of a maverick and had fallen out with the controller, David Hatch, who he referred to on air as 'that silly little man'. Symonds was on borrowed time and was already planning his exit and, like Johnnie Walker before him, heading for California.

His show followed mine on Radio Two in the afternoon. Our studios were divided by a huge glass window, and while I was on air I'd see him preparing his show next door. One afternoon I was reading out some request cards when I looked up to see David's bare bottom pressed up against the window in front of me. Naturally, I started laughing and had to apologise to the people whose card I was reading. "I'm sorry," I said. "I'm not laughing at your names. How can I explain it? Either it's David Symonds next door or there's a full moon tonight."

When I looked up during my next link David was standing on the chair waving his wedding tackle at me and by the link after that he was walking round the studio completely naked. I pressed the talkback and said, "I'll bet you fifty quid you don't do the whole show like that." You're on," said Symonds.

Thus it was that at five o'clock that afternoon David Symonds became Britain's first nude dj. The girls who provided the motoring news were down more than usual that afternoon. It almost came down to delivering messages like "There's a lot of traffic in London tonight." It gave a whole new meaning to the phrase 'motoring flash'.

After about twenty minutes I'd seen enough – literally, so I walked into the studio and gave him the fifty pounds – although he had nowhere to put it. I walked out into the corridor where I bumped into Teddy Warrick, one of Radio One's executives, taking a bunch of Japanese tourists on a tour of the studios. Naturally, being Japanese they were armed with cameras. "Here we have Radio One, the sharp end of the music spectrum," he said. "And round the corner here, Radio Two, which appeals to the more mature listener." Suddenly he caught sight of David Symonds in the buff. "Ah, naturist broadcaster," said one of the Japanese. "You have women who do it as well?"

"No, no, no," said Teddy.

I shall never forgot the sight of Teddy Warrick frantically trying to persuade twenty Japanese tourists to move away from the studio while they all fired away on their cameras. I wonder how many stories were told back in Tokyo about the BBC station in London where dj's broadcast naked.

Chapter 17

THE DJ'S CHRISTMAS PARTY

The day the dj's dreaded more than any other was the station's Christmas party. Held in the governors' dining room at Broadcasting House and hosted by the programme controller's wife, it was the annual event where careers were made or broken. To paranoid and insecure dj's already uncomfortable in dinner jackets and bow ties, the first concern was the seating plan and the fear that their keenest rival was sitting next to the hostess (implying that he was probably her favourite) while they were stuck at the end of the table next to the wife of a dj they couldn't stand.

It was an evening where the wine flowed and tongues loosened. An evening where a dj who'd had a terrible year on air and was earmarked for the push could turn it round by turning on the charm for the hostess. One even offered to babysit her children, an offer she gleefully accepted. Equally, it was an evening when someone who'd been brilliant throughout the year could undo all the good work with one careless remark. Like the man, fortified by some of the Beeb's finest claret, who stood up and made a speech which began, "I wonder how many of us will be here at this time next year." As he sat down to silence, his wife retrieved the situation brilliantly. Taking to her feet she said, "The wives never get to say anything on these occasions. On behalf of us all, I'd like to thank our hostess for arranging such a wonderful evening. I think I can speak for all of us when I say how much we look forward to this dinner every year and how it really is the highlight of our social calendar."

I didn't have a wife at the time so I took a different girlfriend each year, mainly because none of them could hack it more than once. The first year my companion, emerging from the loo at the end of the evening, said to me, "Thanks for the most boring evening of my life." Immediately over her shoulder and definitely within earshot was the programme controller's wife. The following year I took a Japanese girlfriend. When I looked at the table plan I discovered she was sitting next to the controller so I suggested she pretend she didn't understand English and speak only in Japanese all night. Luckily, he didn't understand a word and we chuckled about it all the way home in the taxi. "What did you say to him?" I asked.

"I told him his party was boring and his guests were crap." It was the only party I enjoyed.

Chapter 18

THE RADIO ONE FOOTBALL TEAM

If Noel Edmonds was the only dj to show an aptitude for motor racing, how on earth was Radio One going to send out a football team? As Liverpool and Fulham supporters respectively, John Peel and I were the only ones to have any interest in the sport. Tony Blackburn is the only person I know who could play the game reasonably and yet hate it. Dave Lee Travis wisely elected to be the commentator, but it was worth the admission money to see Simon Bates and Paul Gambaccini running around in football kit. To make up the numbers Teddy Warrick, Derek Chinnery's number two and a Crystal Palace supporter, drafted in song pluggers Alan James and Dave Most and recording star Junior Campbell, formerly of the band Marmalade, the first Scottish band to have a UK number 1, which they did with Paul McCartney's song OB–LA–DI OB–LA–DA.

Despite the abject lack of skill, the team filled football stadiums around the country. When we visited Roker Park, Sunderland were languishing in the old Second Division and ours was the biggest crowd they'd had there all season. Derek Chinnery dropped into the dressing room to wish us luck before we ran out to face our opponents, Radio Newcastle. "Why are they wearing that?" he asked Teddy, pointing at the strip Sunderland had kindly lent us. "They should be wearing Radio One T-shirts". Warrick pointed out that since football was akin to religion on Wearside, in that kit we would be viewed as heroes. Peel and I backed him up and luckily we won the day. Somehow we also managed to win the match.

When the team coach pulled up for a match at Old Trafford we were mobbed by a huge crowd. We discovered later that the size of the turnout probably had something to do with the fact that Bobby Charlton was playing for the other side. Just a few years after he'd stopped playing, Bobby still had all his skills and that rocket shot. It made me wonder why he'd retired so early. The pace of the professional game, I suppose. In the first half he took an in-swinging corner kick with his right foot. It looped over our goalkeeper's head and into the back of the net. One of the dj's told him it was a fluke. "Oh, you think it was a fluke, do you?" said Bobby. So in the second half he took another corner kick, this time with his left foot. Once again it soared into the top of the net. And this time no one said it was a fluke.

Chapter 19

SAVILEGATE

I can't airbrush him out – though I'd like to. He was there – though we rarely saw him. "Now then, now then, guys and gals"; "How's about that then?"; "As it 'appens"; "Goodness, gracious". It was all gobbledegook, wasn't it? What's more, he never physically played a record. He got someone else to do it for him. The mystery is how Jimmy Savile became a top BBC disc-jockey in the first place.

The answer probably lies in the fact that the Beeb, to their shame, never 'discovered' any dj's or gave them their broadcasting debuts. They poached them from someone else, in the early days from Radio Luxembourg and later the pirate stations. In the 1950s Savile had built a reputation as a dance hall dj in the north of England where he claimed to be the first person to use two turntables and a microphone to entertain dancers. This led to him doing sponsored shows for Radio Luxembourg where he launched something he chose to call, not surprisingly, The Teen And Twenty Disc Club. In 1964 he hosted the very first edition of Top Of The Pops from a converted church in Dickenson Road, Manchester. One suspects the reason the BBC chose him was because they saw him as someone who had his finger on the pulse of the nation's youth (which turned out to be even truer than they knew).

Savile came along at a time when disc-jockeys spoke with a 'Standard English' accent. His contemporaries like Pete Murray and David Jacobs had cultured voices, spoke in an intelligent way, were well informed about the music and, particularly in Murray's case, were witty with a good sense of comic timing. If you didn't speak like them, the BBC wouldn't employ you at the time. Then Savile appeared and, with his broad Yorkshire accent, completely broke the mould. He was a showman – once dyeing his hair a new colour every week for a series on Tyne Tees TV – and a brilliant self-publicist and somehow the word got out that he was the hot dj whose work in the dance halls had given the impression that he was a Pied Piper who had the teenagers dancing to his tune. His flamboyant persona was created, no doubt, in his days in the halls when a man playing records with two decks needed something extra to make him a star attraction. As the dance bands became more and more an expensive commodity that few venues could afford, the dj – in effect, a one-man band – was a cheaper option than even the four-man beat groups.

Not long after the launch of Radio One, Jimmy joined with his Savile's Travels, as he toured the country with his caravan and his trusted producer, 'Uncle' Ted Beston. The recorded broadcasts contained plenty of 'nudge nudge, wink wink' remarks as young ladies joined the deadly duo to send their messages to the nation, and listeners were left in little doubt that all sorts of shenanagins were going on behind the curtains. When Savile's Travels ran its course it was replaced by the Old Record Club where Savile rewarded listeners with a number of points for identifying the titles of records and the names of the people who recorded them.

Savile without doubt saw himself as a cut above all the other dj's, though they included huge names like Tony Blackburn and Noel Edmonds. Consequently, he never mixed with any of us and I can't think of a single friend he had among the other jocks. The only time we saw him was at photocalls and press receptions, for example on a big Radio One anniversary. He did once come to a party at the Hampstead home of the Radio One controller, Derek Chinnery. All the dj's were there and Savile was the last to arrive. How did he time it so perfectly? Had he been hiding round the corner waiting to see we were all in the house before he rang the door bell? He came in with the obligatory cigar, dripping in jewellery. "Good evening, young man," he said to each of us, shaking our hands as he made his way towards the controller and his wife, Doreen. It was as though he didn't know any of our names (perhaps he didn't). He walked over to Doreen, showering her arm with kisses, gave Derek 20 minutes of his valuable time and promptly became the first to leave. David 'Kid' Jensen spoke for all of us. "Now royalty has left," he said, "we can have a party." Savile was a master at one-upmanship and no matter how big any of the other stars on the station were, he managed to remain the biggest of all.

Because of his popularity he was often asked to do a daily show and to stand in for regular jocks when they were away. He always turned down the offers, wisely because I'm sure he knew he couldn't cut it. For a start, he had never operated a studio. He was a dj who'd never actually played a record and had always got someone else to play them for him.

When I joined the team of Top Of The Pops in 1975 Savile was already 52, and much older than the other presenters. He looked wrong on the show, but a producer told me, "We could never get rid of Jimmy because he's an institution." "How do you become an institution?" I pondered. Well, Jimmy did it, and he was regarded as unsackable.

I met him again some years later when he'd finally left the BBC. He was doing a syndicated golden oldies show for commercial radio which the bosses at Capital Gold had decided to take. Though Capital didn't produce the show, but bought it in from elsewhere, they wanted to give the impression that Savile was joining their team that included people like Tony Blackburn, Kenny Everett and myself.

Capital Radio at the time was situated in a tower block in Euston Road, on probably the windiest corner in London. The combination of the tower and an underpass in front of it created a vortex so strong that often little old ladies were blown into the road. For Savile's welcoming photocall it was decided to get an attractive young woman to greet him with a glass of champagne (though Savile was teetotal) outside the front doors of the building. Who more obvious to choose for the job than the young blonde working in Capital's press office, Sophie Rhys-Jones (later to marry Prince Edward and become the Duchess of Wessex)? The more the wind blew Sophie's skirt up, the more amorous Jimmy became, showering her arms with kisses. Before long she could stand it no more, storming off back to the press office and saying to her colleagues, "I refuse to have any more pictures taken with that revolting man."

Waiting to do my daily show, I was despatched to the foyer to stand in as the deliverer of champagne. Jimmy's disappointment was palpable. "One minute I have a lovely young lady," he said, "and now a hairy gorilla. What's going on?" I explained that Sophie was feeling ill which, come to think of it, wasn't far from the truth. Savile swept off in the direction of the press office in search of Sophie, who had conveniently disappeared. Undaunted, he then swooped on all the other girls he could find and swamped them all with kisses. Unfortunately, the effect wasn't quite what he had intended, most of them fleeing to the bathroom to wash away any trace of him the moment he left the room.

When Savile died in 2011, I, along with many of my colleagues, was asked to pay tribute to him on BBC and Sky News. I mentioned that he was a 'one off', a showman, and that he did a tremendous amount of good work for charity. I also commented that he was a loner, who didn't mix much with the rest of us, that he led a life that seemed rather lonely but that he did like young ladies. I didn't say 'under-age girls' because I had never seen him with any. I'd heard rumours, but you can't judge someone on the basis of rumours you've heard.

There were two main stories I heard about Savile that came from sources I would normally regard as reliable. The first was about a teenage girl who committed suicide. She kept a diary and in it were stories about 'having sex with Jimmy Savile in his dressing room at the BBC TV centre'. At the time of the entry in the diary the girl was fourteen. I later heard that the News of the World had been shown the diary and were planning to run the story. At the last minute they changed their mind. One could only speculate on the pressure Savile had put on them to drop the revelation.

The other story I heard was of a big campaign Savile fronted to raise money for Stoke Mandeville Hospital. The campaign raised £10 million and Savile's cut was 10%. At a million pounds, working for charity would be far more lucrative for him than any TV or radio work. When questioned about the integrity of taking money intended for charity, Savile said, "So what – without me, they'd never have made the nine million."

I also knew a family in Yorkshire whose teenage daughter spent a lot of time with the dj who would then have been in his forties. Quite often he'd pop round to their house and take her out in his car. Every outing seemed to be with the blessing of the parents. I must say at the time I thought it odd. Blinded by his fame, perhaps.

Whatever stories I heard, because Savile led his life well away from his radio colleagues, I never saw him with under-age girls. If I'd gone to the controller of Radio One and said, "I hear rumours that Jimmy Savile is a paedophile," he'd have said, "How dare you come to me with rumours like that" and probably sacked me on the spot. In fairness to the bosses at the BBC, I'm convinced none of them saw him with young girls, either. If they had, I'm sure they would have taken action against hm. I have to say it was pretty sickening for us to see him get the OBE and then a knighthood when we suspected all along that his charitable good deeds were a cover for a seedy lifestyle.

The Savile scandal exposed him as one of the most prolific paedophiles Britain has ever known, and yet in his lifetime his reputation was untarnished. He conned everyone – the BBC, the hospitals and schools he worked for, the press, even the royal family and the prime minister, Margaret Thatcher, whom he spent Christmases with. He had the reputation of a saint and was untouchable. Only now do we know that he was cunning and crafty and that he used all kinds of artful methods to make sure his sleazy secret didn't come out. The problem with the Savile scandal was that it tarnished everyone who worked alongside him. Newspapers were quick to imply that the Seventies was a seedy decade and that Top Of The Pops was a nasty, sinister show to work on. That's not how I remember it. Though the Seventies were blighted by miners' strikes, high unemployment and rampant inflation, they were a fun time and most of the fun we had was fairly innocent.

It's easy to be wise after the event but looking now at the pictures of Jimmy Savile in his string vests, revolting shell suits and bling jewellery, it's clear how dodgy he looked. My heart goes out to all the people he attacked. How he got away with it all for over six decades is one of life's great mysteries. Jimmy Savile was the all-time con man. He conned us into believing he was a great dj when all he spoke was illiterate nonsense. He showed no interest in the artists whose records he played. How many recording stars owed their breakthrough to him? None that I can think of. He made a huge song and dance about his charity work while almost certainly lining his own pockets from some of the funds hc raised.

What is really amazing is that nothing came out while he was still alive, though clearly he had some narrow escapes. No one will ever know the number of people he abused. Those seeking compensation will find that much of his estate has been soaked up in legal fees. The scrap dealer who bought his Rolls Royce with the number plate JS 247 (the old Radio One wavelength) for £120,000 may have discovered that the plate, if not the car, is worth no more than an addition to his scrap collection. Then there was the woman who paid £22,000 for his bubble car, intending to display it outside her care home in Rotherham. Yes, he let a lot of people down.

For all his fame, he was a lonely man, unable to sustain relationships or friendships. A man who had fans but not friends, who sought the companionship of people who worked in hospitals and charities. None of that excuses his appalling predatory behaviour. He was a man who went through life hiding a dreadful secret. And they gave him Jim'll Fix It.

Sainted in life, tainted in death.

Chapter 20

OUTRO

I am the morning dj on W.O.L.D.
Playing all the hits for you wherever you may be
The bright good morning voice that's heard but never seen
Feeling all of forty- five going on fifteen.

No song better summed up the plight of the ageing dj than Harry Chapin's W.O.L.D.

We all knew it wouldn't last forever which is why we did all the gigs, took all the spin-offs and made the most of it while we could. No wonder few of us were friends. We were too busy looking over our shoulders wondering who was going to take over our slot. The insecurity was personified by the Radio One calendar. Out it came every year and each of the jocks grabbed a copy to find which month he was featured on. December was great. It meant they were planning to have you on the team at the end of the year. Nobody wanted to be Mr January.

And so it came to pass that in time everyone moved on, to be replaced by a new generation of broadcasters – Peter Powell, David 'Kid' Jensen, Mike Read, Paul Gambaccini – and in time they too would give way to a younger bunch. Often change was made just for the sake of change. But where to go after Radio One? The lucky ones were snapped up by Radio Two, although Radio Two didn't want to see itself as a dumping ground for Radio One presenters and resisted some of the overtures that were made to them. Some moved to the commercial stations where they found a form of radio very different from what they had known, dominated by ratings and the need to sell advertising time and run by businessmen prepared to be ruthless and dump a presenter after one poor set of listening figures. Here there was a much quicker turnover of staff and many people who were good at their jobs were dumped purely for economy reasons, which didn't apply at the BBC.

The Radio One of today is very different from how it was in the Seventies. For a start it's no longer the most listened-to station. Since those days Radio Four has developed into a major player but the station with the most listeners is now Radio Two which, if anything, occupies the ground that Radio One held then. Most of the commercial stations struggle to keep up with it. They might be able to play the same music but Radio Two can do it uncluttered by repetitive commercials and with personality dj's like Chris Evans, Ken Bruce and Steve Wright, and of course they can play more music. Listeners would be staggered to find how few records some stations actually play in an hour. Radio One is now going for the younger audience and, whereas the 'class of '76' were known to all age groups, ask people to name the current dj's on Radio One and many will struggle to mention a couple of names.

Things have changed in many ways. When I was at Radio One, using the 'F' word on air was a sackable offence. In recent times it's been heard on the breakfast show by children getting ready for school. I remember Derek Chinnery coming into the studio while I was on air and berating me for a risqué joke I'd told the day before. "I've had complaints about it," he said.

"How many?" I asked.

"Seven."

"Seven among millions of listeners?"

"It's all right for you," he said. "You don't have to answer them."

Commercial radio has changed a lot, too. Capital Radio, originally heard only in London, claimed to be the biggest commercial radio station in Europe. It covers a bigger patch now, being networked to most of the UK and owned by Global Radio, a powerful radio group that has Heart and Smooth as well as the original talk station, LBC, which is also heard on DAB far beyond its original London transmission area. In fact it's now been re-branded from the London Broadcasting Company to 'Leading Britain's Conversation', spearheaded by its breakfast show fronted by the excellent journalist Nick Ferrari.

Magic, owned by Bauer Radio, is another network that grew out of a group of smaller stations around the country. The effect of these networks and the disappearance of the smaller stations is that commercial radio has lost what was its strong point in the first place – its localness. In many cases stations have tried to disguise this by having local breakfast shows but nonetheless the listener is left with the feeling that shows are no longer coming from their neck of the woods but are indeed part of a huge network.

All this has been to the advantage of the BBC local stations which concentrate on the county in which they are based, apart from a networked evening show which was brought in for cost cutting reasons, though whether that really worked is debatable. These stations continue to bring local news, sport and weather and tend to come into their own at times of crisis – e.g. snow, storms and floods.

What has harmed commercial radio more than anything is its narrow playlisting. Some stations have an incredibly small roster of records. Playing the same songs over and over again because they are 'safe' is boring and repetitive. It's hellishly boring for the presenters who have to introduce the same old stuff while trying to sound jolly, and totally predictable to the listeners.

I remember working for one station that had in its repertoire one Queen record, one T Rex and one David Bowie. As soon as I mentioned one of those names, listeners knew which song I was going to play. When you think of all the wonderful records those artistes made, you wonder which music programmer would deny his audience the chance to hear all the others. And yes, today fewer and fewer daytime jocks are allowed to choose their own records. It's all so boring, I wonder how many programme controllers listen to their own stations. In many cases, I'm sure they don't.

Apart from breakfast shows, most commercial stations have done away with 'personality' dj's with the result that on many shows you'll hear anything from three to ten records in a row – Ten at Ten, there's a novel idea. When the dj finally gets to speak, he'll read a liner card (station slogan) or a promo of something the station wants to sell. You could get anybody in off the street to do that. And if you want to hear ten records in a row, you might as well put on a CD. Then you can hear the ten you want, and they won't be interrupted by commercials. People aren't really 'listening' to this kind of radio anymore. It's just something that's on in the background, and they have no idea who the dj is. Never mind, as the Hereward Radios, the 210s, the GWRs and the Red Rose Radios have disappeared, they have been swallowed up by huge networks which are making plenty of money for the owners.

All of this plays brilliantly into the hands of Radio Two as the nation's favourite. And lots of listeners have deserted music radio and opted for the talk stations – Radio Four, Five Live, LBC and TalkSport.

Looking back at the golden days of Radio One, there was a downside as well. Because of our high profiles we were the subject of a great deal of jealousy. Carping newspaper critics said we were bland and overpaid and complained about us plugging our gigs on air. One newspaper ran a feature on the Radio One dj's saying we were all earning more than the prime minister. There was no social media back then so people who were angry took it out on us personally. There were people who scratched our cars. Compering a Rolling Stones concert, I parked my sports car at the back of the venue. Somebody, thinking it was Mick Jagger's car, scratched 'I love you Mick' on the bonnet. Until I had time to get it sprayed I had to drive round with 'I love you Mick' scrawled on my car.

Sometimes it was malicious. I came away from a rock concert and found every panel of the car scratched and the vinyl roof slashed. I once had a swastika sprayed on my car and the word MOD painted on the front door of my house. I never worked out why. I was pelted with hard boiled eggs at a Radio One roadshow and was told it was because of what I'd said about Teddy Boys. For the life of me I couldn't ever remember mentioning them. They'd probably got the wrong dj from the wrong station.

A bunch of students tried to capsize our punt when we were broadcasting on the Cam during a tour of Cambridge and pelted us with flour. The producer's PA looked like a contestant in a wet T-shirt contest. She, the recording engineer and I were lucky not to be dumped in the river along with the recording equipment, which could have been dangerous. The producer, meantime, was 'keeping an eye on things' in the radio van. As a former Cambridge graduate, he probably had an idea of what was coming. Then there was the woman in Yorkshire who told a daily newspaper I'd two-timed her with another woman. I was single at the time and I couldn't see it was much of a story, but it still made the front page. Later I discovered she'd been sleeping with another Radio One dj, who was married.

And there were the stalkers who for some reason seem to home in on radio personalities more than those on television. It must be the magic of the 'one to one medium'. I had my share of stalkers, including the woman who left her husband and children and was sitting on the doorstep outside Broadcasting House with her suitcase, telling me she was going to move in with me.

Another woman looked up my name in the electoral register and threw a brick through a window of my house. Except that it wasn't mine but that of another David Hamilton living in the same area. A few weeks later she turned up at Broadcasting House, ran up behind Paul Burnett (who was unfortunate enough to look a bit like me) and threw a can of yellow paint all over him. "Take that, David Hamilton," she said. "But I'm Paul Burnett," he said, as he whirled round. She got the wrong man twice. When she was arrested by the police and asked why she did it, she said, "He keeps sending me telepathic messages over the radio."

But most of it was fun – playing in charity football matches with Elton John and Rod Stewart, who landed on the pitch in his helicopter, or compering tours with the Bay City Rollers and David Cassidy, who put cotton wool in his ears to stop him hearing the girls screaming, and then couldn't hear the band. It was also fun discovering new talent. During the Seventies I was working on Sunday Night At The London Palladium. I was sitting in the stalls watching rehearsals when on stage came three black girls from Philadelphia singing a song called Year Of Decision. Diana Ross had recently left The Supremes and as I watched and listened to these girls I thought they could be the new Supremes.

The following morning I asked my producer if he'd seen the Palladium Show the night before. When he said, "No," I said, "Well, millions of people did and I think we should have Year Of Decision as our Record of the Week" (the Hamilton Hotshot, as I called it). I promised him it would be a hit, and he agreed to replace the record already planned. The girls were The Three Degrees and, having supported them from the start, it goes without saying that their next record would be a Hamilton Hotshot, too. This was When Will I See You Again. This one went to number 1 and became a multi-million seller around the world so it was a pleasure to present the girls with a Gold Disc on stage at the Victoria Apollo. "I'm here to tell you," I said to the audience, "that When Will I See You Again has sold a million." The crowd went wild. I handed the Gold Disc to Sheila Ferguson, the lead singer, and the band struck up the intro. I listened in the wings as the girls launched into the song that meant so much to so many. They never sang it better. It was a magical evening and I was thrilled to have been part of their success story. Prince Charles later danced with Sheila Ferguson and said the Three Degrees were his favourite group so they became 'by royal appointment'. But I found them first…

Yes, there's no doubt we had the best time – the most listeners, the most fun, the most freedom. And there won't ever be a radio station that has a line-up like Radio One did in 1976. It's fashionable now to rubbish the Seventies dj's and put them all down as being Smashie and Nicey. And, of course, the revelations about Savile have done much to tarnish the decade. But we were the right thing at the time. The world has moved on and radio has moved on with it, but the Sixties and Seventies were the golden era of the dj.

I know you can't bring those times back, but wouldn't it be great to have all those Radio One dj's back together again on one station! A Golden Oldies station on FM like they have in America would clean up. What a wealth of musical knowledge between them all. Mike Read, Paul Burnett, David Kid Jensen, David Symonds. They'd all be there. There might even be a place for me.

I'd like that.

What The Paper Said (about our cover picture)

by Pat Doncaster, Daily Mirror, 19 January 1976

They're the voices you hear first thing in the morning – and last thing at night – the British brand of disc-jockeys. Whenever you switch on to Radio One or Radio Two there they are with their mid-Atlantic voices, used to punctuate records old and new. They seem to spend their lives with one eye on the clock and one finger on the button to start the jingles that give plugs both for them and their programmes. Their main qualification, though, seems to be their ability to chat. For your guidance we present a 'Who's Who' list of the current field of top dj's on the BBC airwaves...

ED STEWART

The 34-year-old Pied Piper of Pop, trailing millions of listening children in his wake, nicknamed Stewpot because "I've always had a slight pot."

Born in Exmouth, Devon. Educated at Oxford. Flew off to Hong Kong to play double bass with a jazz trio, but the contract folded while he was still in the air.

Radio Hong Kong rescued him and he became their rugby reporter and film critic. Home again, he joined the pirates.

A Radio One weekend voice you can trust. He knows how to talk to young people and has time for them.

Parents love him too. Young Mums around the country hold baby's hand to scrawl a postcard request to Ed.

DAVE LEE TRAVIS

30, daily on Radio One in the late afternoon with a programme cryptically entitled, IT'S DLT OK!

From Manchester way where he used to share a council

house with his parents; took the oft-trod road to Broadcasting House via club work and pirate radio.

Tall at the turntable at six feet two and a half and as cheerful as most ("we're all lunatics from up North") he announces without a twinge of shame.

Explaining Radio One's purpose in life he says lightheartedly, "a bit of peace and happiness."

Dave's doing his best although some of the records don't make for that much peace.

ROSKO

The self-styled Emperor with a voice laced with iron filings, 33. Real name Michael Pasternak, son of Hollywood film producer Joe Pasternak.

Educated in Switzerland and Paris. Served in United States Navy, which turned out to be good training for his eventual arrival aboard the good ship Radio Caroline.

Took the name Rosko from an American dj who was his favourite when he was a kid.

The voice can grate but at least he is not pseudo-American and is tolerable most of the time.

Certainly he is a character making it all sound so exciting and important, but keeping the balance with his off-beat humour.

"Send me a stamp with a postcard on it," he says, talking of requests.

ALAN FREEMAN

At 48 one of the elder statesmen of Pop and a pillar of Radio One at weekends.

Born in Melbourne. An accountant way back and paymaster

for Australia's biggest timber company until he came out of the wood to audition for radio in Tasmania and notched up a job as an announcer. Moved on to Australian radio.

Took a world trip in 1957 and stopped off in London. Through the years he has often figured in pet hate-lists. It was once suggested he should be drowned in custard.

What gets up people's noses about Freeman? Too suave, they say. Too smarmy, pompous, overbearing. When criticism is as caustic as that it's a sure sign of success.

ANNE NIGHTINGALE

Anne of the Thousand Ums and Ers – early to mid thirties – a disc person for Radio One on Sunday afternoons.

A journalist from Brighton, graduated into the spin business via disc columns.

Tries to talk too quickly and, as a result, lapses into a sort of oral shorthand that trails away into giggles.

Listeners fall victim of this malaise, sending mail to her 'Daisy Chain' programme feature erroneously addressed to 'Baby Chain' instead.

She explained recently that a request came from Lisbon, Northern Ireland, not, er, Lisbon, Portugal. Can't she say Lisburn, which is the name of the place in Ulster? I mean, would she call Tony Blackburn, Tony Blackbon?

She might well…

JOHN PEEL

36-year-old John Peel was born in West Kirby, Cheshire. Real name John Ravenscroft. Educated Shrewsbury Public School, served two years in the Army.

Wanted to be a journalist, but took himself off to the United

States where he 'bummed around.'

Got his radio introduction via Beatlemania over there. He rang a local dj to correct him on a Beatle item, after which the station phoned John every night.

A station in Oklahoma City snapped him up as a dj almost kidnapping him into the job. Two state patrol cars called unannounced at his digs and whisked him off to the studio.

Moved west to California, then home to be a pirate, approaching the BBC when he was scuttled.

JOHNNIE WALKER

Born Birmingham. Now 30. Educated Solihull Public School. Real name Peter Dingley. Former car salesman. Caroline pirate and club dj.

Worked as labourer between end of pirates and job at the BBC.

Honest in his opinion, but frequently boring with useless information.

Stirred up a controversy when he said the Bay City Rollers served up 'musical rubbish' and told their fans to 'take a running jump at themselves'.

That's the stuff!

TERRY WOGAN

Born in Limerick, raised in Dublin. Without doubt the best voice on radio, caressing the grumbling, stumbling millions into a new day each morn.

He was once caught up in the daily humdrum himself, working in a Dublin bank for five years. Then he saw an advertisement saying Radio Eireann wanted an announcer. He got the job.

Now he has been with us for six years and is a likeable fixture, making war on flab and tipping winning horses (all right, losers).

TONY BLACKBURN

The corny cherub of Radio One, he is 33 this month. A doctor's son and ex-radio pirate, educated at Millfield Public School.

Also went to a singing school and vocalised with dance bands and rock outfits. He made passable records himself, but is far more notorious for his feeble jokes. Recent example: "I'm recovering from a serious accident. I introduced a sailor to a blonde and didn't get out of the way in time. (Tee-hee, chuckle, chuckle.)"

But you have to forgive him. He's nice and wholesome and harmless.

Yet he can be serious when he chooses. Currently he's fed up with the moaners who castigate British television and he promises not to listen to them on radio phone-in programmes any more.

Our TV and radio are wonderful, he says. What's more, he's right.

NOEL EDMONDS

A headmaster's son, public schoolboy (Brentwood College) with ten O-levels and four A-levels. Gave up a university place to be a disc-jockey. Now 27.

Ex-Luxembourg, now a Radio One early bird trying to jolly a large slice of the captive public into consciousness each morning between 7am and 9.

A thankless task with an audience constantly on the move

from bed to bathroom to breakfast, then possibly slamming the door on him to escape to work or school.

Edmonds, a very likeable chap with a smile in his voice, sometimes feels as badly as we do. Words, he revealed one recent morn, were sticking to his mouth.

"But," he joked, "a quick blast with the Radio One blowlamp shifted a few dead words."

He trades in chuckles and puns. Example: "The Leaning Tower of Pisa now has a commissionaire to control the sightseers. Fancy spending your day minding your Pisa queues."

It's just too much. Send for the Radio One pun exterminator!

DAVID HAMILTON

The 35 year-old Casanova of the trannies on Radio One and Two. Educated at Glastonbury Grammar School. Wanted to be a writer or footballer.

Started out as a continuity writer for TV. Got the nickname Diddy (he is 5ft 6in) from Ken Dodd, for whom he once stooged.

Bleaches and tints hair yellow and frequently looks as if he has been hit with a bale of hay and some of it has stuck.

Explains his success thus: "I try to talk to one person. I've got this picture of a woman, a housewife, young or young at heart…"

It works. Thousands of women imagine he is talking to them. One thought he really meant her and rang his doorbell for weeks – and finally landed in court.

WHERE ARE THEY NOW?

See the group photo on the first page of the picture section.

TONY BLACKBURN – *Back on Radio Two with Sounds Of The Sixties and The Golden Hour*

JIMMY YOUNG – *Died 7 November 2016, aged 95*

KENNY EVERETT – *Died 4 April 1995, aged 50*

DUNCAN JOHNSON – *Retired*

ROBIN SCOTT – *Died 7 February, 2000, aged 79*

DAVID RIDER – *Retired, living in Sussex*

DAVE CASH – *Died 21 October 2016, aged 74*

PETE BRADY – *Chief executive of Crystal Clear Film and Video Ltd*

DAVID SYMONDS – *Running an internet radio station from his home in France*

BOB HOLNESS – *Died 6 January 2012, aged 83*

TERRY WOGAN – *Died 31 January 2016, aged 77*

BARRY ALLDIS – *Died in Luxembourg 21 November 1982, aged 52*

MIKE LENNOX – *Returned to his native Canada and working there in property*

KEITH SKUES – *Still broadcasting on BBC Radio Norfolk at age of 78*

CHRIS DENNING – *Serving prison sentence for a string of sexual offences*

JOHNNY MORAN – *Last heard of working for Radio Hallam in Sheffield*

PETE MYERS – *Died 15 December 1998, aged 59*

PETE MURRAY – *Semi-retired, living in Wimbledon, aged 91*

ED STEWART – *Died 9 January 2016, aged 74*

PETE DRUMMOND – *In demand as voice-over artist*

MIKE RAVEN – *Died 4 April 1997, aged 72*

MIKE AHERN – *Died 5 October 2009, aged 67*

JOHN PEEL – *Died 25 October 2004, aged 65*